Swift Essentials

Get up and running lightning fast with this practical guide to building applications with Swift

Dr Alex Blewitt

BIRMINGHAM - MUMBAI

Swift Essentials

First published: December 2014

Production reference: 1201214

Published by Packt Publishing Ltd.
Livery Place
35 Livery Street
Birmingham B3 2PB, UK.

ISBN 978-1-78439-670-1

www.packtpub.com

Credits

Author

Dr Alex Blewitt

Reviewers

Nate Cook

Arvid Gerstmann

James Robert

Anil Varghese

Commissioning Editor

Sarah Crofton

Acquisition Editor

Sam Wood

Content Development Editor

Arwa Manasawala

Technical Editor

Faisal Siddiqui

Copy Editors

Dipti Kapadia

Shambhavi Pai

Project Coordinator

Danuta Jones

Proofreaders

Simran Bhogal

Ameesha Green

Paul Hindle

Indexer

Rekha Nair

Production Coordinator

Alwin Roy

Cover Work

Alwin Roy

About the Author

Dr Alex Blewitt has over 20 years of experience in Objective-C and has been using Apple frameworks since NeXTSTEP 3.0. He upgraded his NeXTstation for a TiBook when Apple released Mac OS X in 2001 and has been developing on it ever since.

Alex currently works for a financial company in London and writes for the online technology news site InfoQ. He has authored two other books for Packt Publishing. He also has a number of apps on the App Store through Bandlem Limited. When he's not working on technology and the weather is nice, he likes to go flying from the nearby Cranfield airport.

Alex writes regularly on his blog `http://alblue.bandlem.com` as well tweets regularly on Twitter, `@alblue`.

Acknowledgments

This book would not have been possible without the ongoing love and support of my wife, Amy, who has helped me through the highs and lows of life. She gave me the freedom to work during the many late nights and weekends that it takes to produce a book and its associated code repository. She truly is the gem of my life.

I'd also like to thank my parents, Ann and Derek, for their encouragement and support during my formative years. It was their work ethics that allowed me to start my career in technology as a teenager and to incorporate my first company before I was 25. I'd also like to congratulate them on their 50th wedding anniversary in 2015, and I look forward to reaching this milestone with Amy.

Thanks is due especially to the reviewers of the book, Nate Cook, James Robert, Arvid Gerstmann, and Anil Varghese, who provided excellent feedback on the contents of this book during development and caught many errors in both the text and code. Any remaining errors are my own.

I'd also like to thank CodeClub, with whom I have been volunteering to teach young children how to code, and Akeley Wood, for allowing me to be a part of it. I hope both Sam and Holly enjoy it as much as I do.

Finally, I'd like to thank Ben Moseley and Eren Kotan who introduced me to NeXT in the first place and set my career going on a twenty-year journey to this book.

About the Reviewers

Nate Cook is an independent web and application developer who works on projects of all sizes, from websites and blogs for non profit organizations to customized Enterprise applications for Fortune 500 companies. He frequently writes about topics in Swift at http://www.natecook.com/blog.

Arvid Gerstmann is a 20-year-old software developer with a strong interest in mobile platforms and game development. He started experimenting with software development around 2006 and is one of the early adopters of the mobile age. Currently, he lives in Hamburg, Germany, and works as a lead developer in a company focused on mobile applications and games.

You can find him at http://arvid-gerstmann.de.

James Robert is a technologist who follows his curiosity. He's the CTO of Media Predict and a maintainer of several open source projects, including Pydub, which is an open source audio processing library. He's also the cohost of the Biz vs Dev podcast and writes about technology under the moniker "jiaaro."

Anil Varghese is an enthusiastic software engineer from Kerala, India, who is currently focusing on iOS application development. He is constantly striving to learn new technologies and learn better and faster ways to solve problems. He is keenly looking forward to working with the future of iOS, Swift. He always finds time to help fellow programmers and is an active member of developer communities, such as Stack Overflow (`http://stackoverflow.com/users/2021193/anil`).

You can contact him at `anilvarghese@icloud.com`.

www.PacktPub.com

Support files, eBooks, discount offers, and more

For support files and downloads related to your book, please visit www.PacktPub.com.

Did you know that Packt offers eBook versions of every book published, with PDF and ePub files available? You can upgrade to the eBook version at www.PacktPub. com and as a print book customer, you are entitled to a discount on the eBook copy. Get in touch with us at service@packtpub.com for more details.

At www.PacktPub.com, you can also read a collection of free technical articles, sign up for a range of free newsletters and receive exclusive discounts and offers on Packt books and eBooks.

https://www2.packtpub.com/books/subscription/packtlib

Do you need instant solutions to your IT questions? PacktLib is Packt's online digital book library. Here, you can search, access, and read Packt's entire library of books.

Why subscribe?

- Fully searchable across every book published by Packt
- Copy and paste, print, and bookmark content
- On demand and accessible via a web browser

Free access for Packt account holders

If you have an account with Packt at www.PacktPub.com, you can use this to access PacktLib today and view 9 entirely free books. Simply use your login credentials for immediate access.

Table of Contents

Preface

Swift Essentials provides an overview of the Swift language and the tooling necessary to write iOS applications. From simple Swift commands on the command line to interactively testing graphical content in the Playground editor, the Swift language and syntax is introduced by examples.

The book also introduces end-to-end iOS application development by showing you how a simple iOS application can be created, followed by how to use storyboards and custom views to build a more complex networked application.

The book concludes by providing a worked example from scratch that builds up a GitHub repository browser.

What this book covers

Chapter 1, Exploring Swift, presents the Swift read-evaluate-print-loop (REPL) and introduces the Swift language through examples on standard data types, functions, and looping.

Chapter 2, Playing with Swift, demonstrates Swift Playgrounds as a means to interactively play with the Swift code and obtain graphical results. It also introduces the playground format and shows how playgrounds can be created automatically from Markdown and AsciiDoc files.

Chapter 3, Creating an iOS Swift App, shows you how to create and test an iOS application built in Swift using Xcode, along with an overview of the Swift classes, protocols, and enums.

Chapter 4, Storyboard Applications with Swift and iOS, introduces the concept of Storyboards as a means to create a multiscreen iOS application and shows how views in Interface Builder can be wired to Swift outlets and actions.

Chapter 5, Creating Custom Views in Swift, covers custom views in Swift using custom table views, laying out nested views, drawing custom graphics, and layered animations.

Chapter 6, Parsing Networked Data, demonstrates how Swift can talk to networked services, using both HTTP and custom stream-based protocols.

Chapter 7, Building a Repository Browser, uses the techniques described in this book to build a repository browser that can display information about users' GitHub repositories.

Appendix provides additional references and resources to continue learning about Swift.

What you need for this book

The exercises in this book are written and tested for Swift 1.1, which is bundled with Xcode 6.1. To run the exercises, you need to have a Mac OS X computer running 10.9 or above with Xcode 6.1 or higher. If newer versions of Swift are released, check the book's GitHub repository or the book's errata page at PacktPub for details about any changes that might affect the book's content.

Xcode can be installed via the App Store as a free download; search for Xcode in the search box. Alternatively, Xcode can be downloaded from `https://developer.apple.com/xcode/downloads/`, which is referenced from the iOS Developer Center at `https://developer.apple.com/devcenter/ios/`.

Once Xcode is installed, it can be launched from `/Applications/Xcode.app` or from Finder. To run the command-line based exercises, Terminal can be launched from `/Applications/Utilities/Terminal.app`, and if Xcode is installed successfully, Swift can be launched by running `xcrun swift`.

The iOS applications can be developed and tested in the iOS simulator that comes bundled with Xcode. It is not necessary to have an iOS device to write or test code. However, if you want to run the code on an iOS device, then you need to join the iOS developer program. More information is available at `https://developer.apple.com/programs/ios/`.

Who this book is for

This book is aimed at developers who are interested in learning the Swift programming language and how to write iOS applications using Swift. No prior programming experience for iOS is assumed, although a basic level of programming experience in a dynamically or statically typed programming language is expected. It is assumed that you are familiar with navigating and using Mac OS X and in the cases where Terminal commands are required, you have experience of simple shell commands or can pick them up quickly from the examples given.

Developers who are familiar with Objective-C will know many of the frameworks and libraries mentioned; however, an existing knowledge of Objective-C and its frameworks is neither necessary nor assumed.

The sources are provided in a GitHub repository at `https://github.com/alblue/com.packtpub.swift.essentials/` and can be used to switch between the content of chapters using the tags in the repository. A knowledge of Git is helpful if you want to navigate between different versions; alternatively, the web-based interface at GitHub can be used instead. It is highly recommended that you become familiar with Git, as it is the standard version control system for Xcode and the de facto standard for open source projects. You are invited to read the Git topics at the author's blog, `http://alblue.bandlem.com/Tag/git/`, if you are unfamiliar and interested in learning more.

Trademarks

GitHub is a trademark of GitHub Inc., and the examples in this book have not been endorsed, reviewed, or approved by GitHub Inc. Mac and OS X are trademarks of Apple Inc., registered in the U.S. and other countries. iOS is a trademark or registered trademark of Cisco in the U.S. and other countries and is used under license.

Conventions

In this book, you will find a number of styles of text that distinguish between different kinds of information. Here are some examples of these styles and an explanation of their meaning.

Code words in text, database table names, folder names, filenames, file extensions, pathnames, dummy URLs, user input, and Twitter handles are shown as follows: "We can include other contexts through the use of the `include` directive."

A block of code is set as follows:

```
@IBInspectable var progressAmount: CGFloat = 0.5 {
    didSet {
        setNeedsLayout()
    }
}
```

When we wish to draw your attention to a particular part of a code block, the relevant lines or items are set in bold:

```
case "entry":
inEntry = true
case "link":
link = attributes.objectForKey("href") as String?
default break;
```

Any command-line input or output is written as follows:

```
# cp /usr/src/asterisk-addons/configs/cdr_mysql.conf.sample
    /etc/asterisk/cdr_mysql.conf
```

New terms and **important words** are shown in bold. Words that you see on the screen, in menus or dialog boxes for example, appear in the text like this: "Clicking the **Next** button moves you to the next screen."

 Warnings or important notes appear in a box like this.

 Tips and tricks appear like this.

Reader feedback

Feedback from our readers is always welcome. Let us know what you think about this book—what you liked or may have disliked. Reader feedback is important for us to develop titles that you really get the most out of.

To send us general feedback, simply send an e-mail to feedback@packtpub.com, and mention the book title via the subject of your message.

If there is a topic that you have expertise in and you are interested in either writing or contributing to a book, see our author guide on www.packtpub.com/authors.

Customer support

Now that you are the proud owner of a Packt book, we have a number of things to help you to get the most from your purchase.

Downloading the example code

You can download the example code files for all Packt books you have purchased from your account at http://www.packtpub.com. If you purchased this book elsewhere, you can visit http://www.packtpub.com/support and register to have the files e-mailed directly to you.

Errata

Although we have taken every care to ensure the accuracy of our content, mistakes do happen. If you find a mistake in one of our books—maybe a mistake in the text or the code—we would be grateful if you would report this to us. By doing so, you can save other readers from frustration and help us improve subsequent versions of this book. If you find any errata, please report them by visiting http://www.packtpub.com/submit-errata, selecting your book, clicking on the **errata submission form** link, and entering the details of your errata. Once your errata are verified, your submission will be accepted and the errata will be uploaded on our website, or added to any list of existing errata, under the Errata section of that title. Any existing errata can be viewed by selecting your title from http://www.packtpub.com/support.

Piracy

Piracy of copyright material on the Internet is an ongoing problem across all media. At Packt, we take the protection of our copyright and licenses very seriously. If you come across any illegal copies of our works, in any form, on the Internet, please provide us with the location address or website name immediately so that we can pursue a remedy.

Please contact us at `copyright@packtpub.com` with a link to the suspected pirated material.

We appreciate your help in protecting our authors, and our ability to bring you valuable content.

Questions

You can contact us at `questions@packtpub.com` if you are having a problem with any aspect of the book, and we will do our best to address it.

1
Exploring Swift

Apple announced Swift at WWDC 2014 as a new programming language that combines experience with the Objective-C platform and advances in dynamic and statically typed languages over the last few decades. Before Swift, most code written for iOS and OS X applications was in Objective-C, a set of object-oriented extensions to the C programming language. Swift aims to build upon patterns and frameworks of Objective-C but with a more modern runtime and automatic memory management.

This chapter will present the following topics:

- How to use the Swift REPL to evaluate Swift code
- The different types of Swift literals
- How to iterate through arrays, dictionaries, and sequences
- Functions and the different types of function arguments
- Compiling and running Swift from the command line

Getting started with Swift

Swift provides a runtime interpreter that executes statements and expressions. The Swift interpreter is called **swift** and can be launched from the Xcode 6 tools using the **xcrun** command in a `Terminal.app` shell:

```
$ xcrun swift
Welcome to Swift!  Type :help for assistance.
>
```

The `xcrun` command allows a toolchain command to be executed; in this case, it finds `/Applications/Xcode.app/Contents/Developer/Toolchains/XcodeDefault.xctoolchain/usr/bin/swift`. The `swift` command sits alongside other compilation tools such as `clang` and `ld`, and permits multiple versions of the commands and libraries to be installed on the same machine without conflicting. The Swift prompt displays > for new statements and . for continuation. Statements and expressions typed into the interpreter are evaluated and immediately displayed. Anonymous values are given references, so they can be used subsequently:

```
> "Hello " +
. "World"
$R0: String = "Hello World"
> 3 + 4
$R1: Int = 7
> $R0
$R2: String = "Hello World"
> $R1
$R3: Int = 7
```

Numeric literals

Numeric types in Swift can represent both signed and unsigned integral values with sizes 8, 16, 32, or 64 bits, as well as signed 32 or 64 bit floating point values. Numbers can include underscores to provide better readability; so `68_040` is the same as `68040`:

```
> 3.141
$R0: Double = 3.141
> 299_792_458
$R1: Int = 299792458
> -1
$R2: Int = -1
> 1_800_123456
$R3: Int = 1800123456
```

Numbers can also be written in **binary, octal,** or **hexadecimal** using prefixes `0b`, `0o` (zero and the letter "o") or `0x`. Note that Swift does not inherit C's use of a leading zero (0) to represent an octal value, unlike Java and JavaScript which do. Examples include:

```
> 0b1010011
$R0: Int = 83
> 0o123
$R1: Int = 83
> 0123
```

```
$R2: Int = 123
> 0x7b
$R3: Int = 123
```

Floating point literals

There are three types of floating point values available in Swift, which use the **IEEE754** floating point standard. The Double type represents 64 bits worth of data whilst Float stores 32 bits of data. In addition, Float80 is a specialized type that stores 80 bits worth of data.

 Some CPUs internally use 80 bit precision to perform math operations, and the Float80 type allows this accuracy to be used in Swift. Not all architectures support Float80 natively, so this should be used sparingly.

By default, floating point values in Swift have the Double type. As floating point representation cannot represent some numbers exactly, some values will be displayed with a rounding error; for example:

```
> 3.141
$R0: Double = 3.141
> Float(3.141)
$R1: Float = 3.1400003
```

Floating point values can be specified in decimal or hexadecimal. Decimal floating point uses e as the exponent for base 10, whereas hexadecimal floating point uses p as the exponent for base 2. A value of AeB has the value A*10^B and a value of 0xApB has the value A*2^B:

```
> 299.792458e6
$R0: Double = 299792458
> 299.792_458_e6
$R1: Double = 299792458
> 0x1p8
$R2: Double = 256
> 0x1p10
$R3: Double = 1024
> 0x4p10
$R4: Double = 4096
> 1e-1
$R5: Double = 0.1000000000000001
> 1e-2
```

```
$R6: Double = 0.01
> 0x1p-1
$R7: Double = 0.5
> 0x1p-2
$R8: Double = 0.25
> 0xAp-1
$R9: Double = 5
```

String literals

Strings can contain escaped characters, unicode characters, and interpolated expressions. Escaped characters use a slash (\) and can be one of:

- \\ Literal slash \
- \0 The null character
- \' Literal single quote '
- \" Literal double quote "
- \t Tab
- \n Line feed
- \r Carriage return
- \u{NNN} Unicode character such as the Euro symbol \u{20AC} or smiley \u{1F600}

An **interpolated string** has an embedded expression which is evaluated, converted into a string, and concatenated into the result. These interpolated strings can capture local variables or expressions:

```
> "3+4 is \(3+4)"
$R0: String = "3+4 is 7"
> 3+4
$R1: Int = 7
> "7 x 2 is \($R1 * 2)"
$R2: String = "7 x 2 is 14"
```

Expressions in interpolated strings cannot contain double quotes. If the expression requires double quotes, assign the value to a constant first and then use that constant in the interpolated string.

Variables and constants

Swift distinguishes between variables (which can be modified) and constants (which cannot be changed after assignment). Identifiers start with an underscore or alphabetic letter, followed by an underscore or alphanumeric character. In addition, other Unicode character points (such as emoji) can be used, although box lines and arrows are not allowed. Consult the Swift language guide for the full set of allowable Unicode characters. Generally, private use areas are not allowed and identifiers cannot start with a combining character (such as an accent).

Variables are defined with the `var` keyword and constants are defined with the `let` keyword. If the types are not specified, they are automatically inferred:

```
> let pi = 3.141
pi: Double = 3.141
> pi = 3
error: cannot assign to 'let' value 'pi'
> var i = 0
i: Int = 0
> ++i
$R0: Int = 1
```

Types can be explicitly specified. For example, to store a 32 bit floating point value, the variable can be defined as a `Float`, or to store a value as an unsigned 8 bit integer, `UInt8`:

```
> let e:Float = 2.718
e: Float = 2.71799994
> let ff:UInt8 = 255
ff: UInt8 = 255
```

To convert a number to a different type, it can be converted using the type initializer or assigned to a variable of a different type, provided it does not underflow or overflow:

```
> let ooff = UInt16(ff)
ooff: UInt16 = 255
> Int8(255)
error: integer overflows when converted from 'Int' to 'Int8'
Int8(255)
^
> UInt8(Int8(-1))
error: negative integer cannot be converted to unsigned type 'UInt8'
UInt8(Int8(-1))
^
```

Collection types

Swift has two collection types: **Array** and **Dictionary**. They are strongly typed and generic, which ensures that the values of types assigned are compatible with the element type. The literal syntax for arrays uses `[]` to store a comma-separated list, while dictionaries use a comma-separated `[key:value]` format for entries. Collections defined with `var` are mutable; collections defined with `let` are immutable.

```
> var shopping = [ "Milk", "Eggs", "Coffee", ]
shopping: [String] = 3 values {
    [0] = "Milk"
    [1] = "Eggs"
    [2] = "Coffee"
}
> var costs = [ "Milk":1, "Eggs":2, "Coffee":3, ]
costs: [String : Int] = {
    [0] = { key = "Coffee" value = 3 }
    [1] = { key = "Milk"   value = 1 }
    [2] = { key = "Eggs"   value = 2 }
}
```

 For readability, array and dictionary literals can have a trailing comma. This allows initialization to be split over multiple lines, and if the last element ends with a trailing comma, adding new items does not result in an SCM diff to the previous line.

Arrays and dictionaries can be indexed using subscript operators, reassigned, and added to as follows:

```
> shopping[0]
$R0: String = "Milk"
> costs["Milk"]
$R1: Int? = 1
> shopping.count
$R2: Int = 3
> shopping += [ "Tea" ]
> shopping.count
$R3: Int = 4
> costs.count
$R4: Int = 3
> costs["Tea"] = "String"
error: '@lvalue $T5' is not identical to '(String, Int)'
```

```
> costs["Tea"] = 4
> costs.count
$R5: Int = 4
```

Optional types

In the previous example, the return type of `costs["Milk"]` is `Int?` and not `Int`. This is an **optional type**; it represents the possibility of an `Int` existing. For a dictionary of type `T`, the return type will be `T?`. If the value doesn't exist in the dictionary, then the returned value will be `nil`. Other object-oriented languages, such as Objective-C, C++, Java, and C#, have optional types by default; any object value (or pointer) can be `null`. By expressing optionality in the type system, Swift can determine whether a value really has to exist or might be `nil`:

```
> var cannotBeNil:Int = 1
cannotBeNil: Int = 1
> cannotBeNil = nil
error: type 'Int' does not conform to protocol 'NilLiteralConvertible'
cannotBeNil = nil
> var canBeNil:Int? = 1
canBeNil: Int? = 1
> canBeNil = nil
> canBeNil
$R0: Int? = nil
```

 Optional types can be explicitly created using the `Optional` constructor. Given a value x of type X, an optional X? value can be created using `Optional(x)`.

The value can be tested against `nil` to find out whether it contains a value and then unpacked with `opt!`.

As an example, here is how to create and unwrap an optional value:

```
> var opt: Int? = 1
opt: Int? = 1
> opt == nil
$R1: Bool = false
> opt!
$R2: Int = 1
```

If a `nil` value is unpacked, an error occurs:

```
> opt = nil
> opt!
fatal error: unexpectedly found nil while unwrapping an Optional value
Execution interrupted. Enter Swift code to recover and continue.
Enter LLDB commands to investigate (type :help for assistance.)
```

Particularly when working with Objective-C based APIs, it is common for values to be declared as optional, although they are always expected to return a value. It is possible to declare such variables as **implicitly unwrapped optionals**; these variables behave as optional values (they may contain `nil`), but when the value is accessed, they are automatically unwrapped on demand:

```
> var implicitlyUnwrappedOptional:Int! = 1
implicitlyUnwrappedOptional: Int! = 1
> implicitlyUnwrappedOptional + 2
3
> implicitlyUnwrappedOptional = nil
> implicitlyUnwrappedOptional + 2
fatal error: unexpectedly found nil while unwrapping an Optional value
```

In general, implicitly unwrapped optionals should be avoided as they are likely to lead to errors. They are mainly useful for interaction with existing Objective-C APIs when the value is known to have an instance.

Nil coalescing operator

Swift has a **nil coalescing operator**, which is similar to Groovy's `?:` operator or C#'s `??` operator. This provides a means to specify a default value if an expression is `nil`:

```
> 1 ?? 2
$R0: Int = 1
> nil ?? 2
$R1: Int = 2
```

The nil coalescing operator can also be used to unwrap an optional value. If the optional value is present, it is unwrapped and returned; if it is missing, then the right-hand side of the expression is returned. Like the shortcut || and && operators, the right-hand side is not evaluated unless necessary:

```
> costs["Tea"] ?? 0
$R2: Int = 4
> costs["Sugar"] ?? 0
$R3: Int = 0
```

Conditional logic

There are two key types of conditional logic in Swift (known as branch statements in the grammar): the if statement and the switch statement. Unlike other languages, the body of the if must be surrounded with braces {}, and if typed in at the interpreter, the opening brace { must be on the same line as the if statement. The literal values true and false can be used as well as other boolean expressions.

If statements

Conditionally unpacking an optional value is so common that a specific Swift pattern has been created to avoid evaluating the expression twice:

```
var shopping = [ "Milk", "Eggs", "Coffee", "Tea", ]
var costs = [ "Milk":1, "Eggs":2, "Coffee":3, "Tea":4, ]
var cost = 0
if let cm = costs["Milk"] {
.    cost += cm
. }
> cost
$R0: Int = 1
```

The if block only executes if the optional value exists. The definition of the constant cm only exists for the body of the if block, and does not exist outside that scope. Furthermore, cm is a non-optional type, so it is guaranteed to not be nil.

To execute an alternative block if the item cannot be found, an `else` block can be used:

```
> if let cb = costs["Bread"] {
.   cost += cb
. } else {
.   println("Cannot find any Bread")
. }
Cannot find any Bread
```

Other boolean expressions can include any expression that conforms to the `BooleanType` protocol, the equality operators `==` and `!=`, the identity operators `===` and `!==`, as well as the comparison operators `<`, `<=`, `>`, `>=`. The `is` type operator provides a test to see whether an element is of a particular type.

> The difference between the **equality operator** and the **identity operator** is relevant for classes or other reference types. The equality operator asks "Are these two values equivalent to each other?" whereas the identity operator asks "Are these two references equal to each other?"

There is a boolean operator specific to Swift, which is the `~=` **pattern match operator**. Despite the name, this isn't anything to do with regular expressions; rather, it's a way of asking whether a pattern matches a particular value. This is used in the implementation of the `switch` block, which is covered in the next section.

In addition to the `if` statement, there is a **ternary if expression** similar to other languages. After a condition, a question mark (`?`) is used, followed by an expression to be used if the condition is true, then a colon (`:`) followed by the false expression:

```
> var i = 17
i: Int = 17
> i % 2 == 0 ? "Even" : "Odd"
$R0: String = "Odd"
```

Switch statements

In addition to if/else, Swift also has a switch statement, similar to C and Java's switch. However, it differs in two important ways. Firstly, case statements no longer have a default fall-through behavior (so there are no bugs introduced by missing a break statement) and secondly, the value of the case statements can be expressions instead of values, pattern matching on type and range. At the end of the corresponding case, the evaluation jumps to the end of the switch block, unless the fallthrough keyword is used. If no case statements match, the default statement is executed:

```
> var position = 21
position: Int = 21
> switch position {
.    case 1: println("First")
.    case 2: println("Second")
.    case 3: println("Third")
.    case 4...20: println("\(position)th")
.    case position where (position % 10) == 1:
.      println("\(position)st")
.    case let p where (p % 10) == 2:
.      println("\(p)nd")
.    case let p where (p % 10) == 3:
.      println("\(p)rd")
.    default: println("\(position)th")
. }
21st
```

In the preceding example, the expression prints out First, Second, or Third if the position is 1, 2, or 3 respectively. For numbers between 4 and 20 (inclusive), it prints out the position with a th ordinal. Otherwise, for numbers that end with 1, it prints st; for numbers that end with 2, it prints nd; and for numbers that end with 3, it prints rd. For all other numbers, it prints th.

The `4...20` range expression in a case statement represents a pattern. If the value of the expression matches that pattern, then the corresponding statements will be executed:

```
> 4...10 ~= 4
$R0: Bool = true
> 4...10 ~= 21
$R1: Bool = false
```

There are two range operators in Swift: an inclusive or **closed range**, and an exclusive or **half-open range**. The closed range is specified with three dots; `1...12` will give a list of integers between one and twelve. The half-open range is specified with two dots and a less than operator; so `1..<10` will provide integers from 1 to 9 but exclude 10.

The `where` clause in the `switch` block allows an arbitrary expression to be evaluated, provided that the pattern matches. These are evaluated in-order, in the sequence they are in the source file. If a `where` clause evaluates to `true`, then the corresponding set of statements will be executed.

The `let` variable syntax can be used to define a constant that refers to the value in the `switch` block. This local constant can be used in the `where` clause or the corresponding statements for that specific case. Alternatively, variables can be used from the surrounding scope.

If multiple `case` statements need to match the same pattern, they can be separated with commas in the form of an expression list. Alternatively, the `fallthrough` keyword can be used to allow the same implementation to be used for multiple `case` statements.

Iteration

Ranges can be used to iterate a fixed number of times, for example, `for i in 1...12`. To print out these numbers, a loop such as the following can be used:

```
> for i in 1...12 {
.    println("i is \(i)")
. }
```

If the number is not required, then the underscore (_) can be used as a hole to act as a throwaway value. An underscore can be assigned to, but not read:

```
> for _ in 1...12 {
.    println("Looping...")
. }
```

However, it is more common to iterate over a collection's contents using a `for...in` pattern. This steps through each of the items in the collection, and the body of the `for` loop is executed over each one:

```
> var shopping = [ "Milk", "Eggs", "Coffee", "Tea", ]
> var costs = [ "Milk":1, "Eggs":2, "Coffee":3, "Tea":4, ]
> var cost = 0
> for item in shopping {
.   if let itemCost = costs[item] {
.     cost += itemCost
.   }
. }
> cost
cost: Int = 10
```

To iterate over a dictionary, it is possible to extract the keys or the values and process them as an array:

```
> Array(costs.keys)
$R2: [String] = 4 values {
  [0] = "Coffee"
  [1] = "Milk"
  [2] = "Eggs"
  [3] = "Tea"
}
> Array(costs.values)
$R3: [Int] = 4 values {
  [0] = 3
  [1] = 1
  [2] = 2
  [3] = 4
}
```

Note that the order of keys in a dictionary are not guaranteed; if the dictionary changes size, the order may change.

Converting a dictionary's values to an array is not performant, as this will result in a copy of the data being made. Instead, the underlying values are of a type `MapCollectionView`, which provides an iterable internal view of the data structure:

```
> costs.keys
$R4: LazyBidirectionalCollectionMapCollectionView<[String : Int],
String>> = {
  _base = {
    _base = {
      [0] = { key = "Coffee" value = 3 }
      [1] = { key = "Milk"   value = 1 }
      [2] = { key = "Eggs"   value = 2 }
      [3] = { key = "Tea"    value = 4 }
    }
  _transform =
    }
}
```

To print out all the keys in a dictionary, the `keys` property can be used with a `for...in` loop:

```
> for item in costs.keys {
. println(item)
. }
Coffee
Milk
Eggs
Tea
```

Iterating over keys and values in a dictionary

Traversing a dictionary to obtain all of the keys and then subsequently looking up values will result in searching the data structure twice. Instead, both the key and the value can be iterated at the same time using a **tuple**. A tuple is like a fixed-sized array, but one that allows assigning pairs (or triplets and so on) of values at a time:

```
> var (a,b) = (1,2)
a: Int = 1
b: Int = 2
```

Tuples can be used to iterate pairwise over both the keys and values of a dictionary:

```
> for (item,cost) in costs {
.   println("The \(item) costs \(cost)")
. }
The Coffee costs 3
The Milk costs 1
The Eggs costs 2
The Tea costs 4
```

Both `Array` and `Dictionary` conform to the **SequenceType** protocol, which allows them to be iterated with a `for...in` loop. Collections (as well as other objects such as `Range`) that implement `SequenceType` have a `generate` method, which returns a `GeneratorType` that allows the data to be iterated over. It is possible for custom Swift objects to implement `SequenceType` to allow them to be used in a `for...in` loop.

Iteration with for loops

Although the most common use of the `for` operator in Swift is in a `for...in` loop, it is also possible to use a more traditional form of `for` loop. This has an initialization, a condition that is tested at the start of each loop, and a step operation that is evaluated at the end of each loop. Although the parentheses around the `for` loop are optional, the braces for the block of code are mandatory.

Calculating the sum of integers between 1 and 10 without using the range operator can be done as follows:

```
> var sum = 0
. for var i=0; i<=10; ++i {
.   sum += i
. }
sum: Int = 55
```

If multiple variables need to be updated in the `for` loop, Swift has an **expression list** that is a set of comma-separated expressions. To step through two sets of variables in a for loop, the following can be used:

```
> for var i = 0,j = 10; i<=10 && j >= 0; ++i,--j {
.   println("\(i), \(j)")
. }
0, 10
1, 9
...
9, 1
10, 0
```

Apple recommends the use of `++i` instead of `i++` (and conversely, `--i` instead of `i--`) because they will return the result of `i` after the operation, which may be the expected value.

Break and continue

The `break` statement leaves the innermost loop early, and control jumps to the end of the loop. The `continue` statement takes execution to the top of the innermost loop and the next item.

To `break` or `continue` from nested loops, a **label** can be used. Labels in Swift can only be applied to a loop statement such as `while` or `for`. A label is introduced by an identifier and a colon just before the loop statement:

```
> var deck = [1...13, 1...13, 1...13, 1...13]
> suits: for suit in deck {
.   for card in suit {
.     if card == 3 {
.       continue // go to next card in same suit
.     }
.     if card == 5 {
.       continue suits // go to next suit
.     }
.     if card == 7 {
.       break // leave card loop
```

```
.   }
.   if card == 13 {
.       break suits // leave suit loop
.   }
.   }
. }
```

Functions

Functions can be created using the `func` keyword, which takes a set of arguments and a body that can be invoked. The `return` statement can be used to leave a function:

```
> var shopping = [ "Milk", "Eggs", "Coffee", "Tea", ]
> var costs = [ "Milk":1, "Eggs":2, "Coffee":3, "Tea":4, ]
> func costOf(items:[String], costs:[String:Int]) -> Int {
.   var cost = 0
.   for item in items {
.     if let cm = costs[item] {
.       cost += cm
.     }
.   }
.   return cost
. }
> costOf(shopping,costs)
$R0: Int = 10
```

The return type of the function is specified after the arguments with an arrow (`->`). If missing, the function cannot return a value; if present, the function must return a value of that type.

Functions with **positional arguments** can be called with parentheses, such as the `costOf(shopping,costs)` call. If a function takes no arguments, then the parentheses are still required.

 The `foo()` expression calls the function `foo` with no arguments. The expression `foo` is the function itself, so an expression such as `let copyOfFoo = foo` results in a copy of the function; so `copyOfFoo()` and `foo()` have the same effect.

Named arguments

Swift also supports **named arguments**, which can either use the name of the variable or can be defined with an **external parameter name**. To modify the function to support calling with `basket` and `prices` as argument names, the following can be done:

```
> func costOf(basket items:[String], prices costs:[String:Int]) -> Int
{
.    var cost = 0
.    for item in items {
.      if let cm = costs[item] {
.        cost += cm
.      }
.    }
.    return cost
. }
> costOf(basket:shopping, prices:costs)
$R1: Int = 10
```

This example defines external parameter names `basket` and `prices` for the function. The function signature is often referred to as `costOf(basket:prices:)` and is useful when it may not be clear what the arguments are for (particularly if they are for the same type).

A shorthand is available to use the same external name as the parameter name, by prefixing it with a hash (#). These are called **shorthand external parameter names**:

```
> func costOf(#items:[String], #costs:[String:Int]) -> Int {
. var cost = 0
. for item in items {
.   if let cm = costs[item] {
.     cost += cm
.   }
. }
. return cost
. }
> costOf(items:shopping, costs:costs)
$R2: Int = 10
```

Refactoring shorthand external parameter names will lead to API breakage. If it is necessary to change the name internally in a function, convert it from a shorthand name to a separate external and internal parameter name.

Optional arguments and default values

Swift functions can have **optional arguments** by specifying **default values** in the function definition. When the function is called and an optional argument is missing, the default value for that argument is used.

> Note that an optional argument is one that can be omitted in the function call, rather than a required argument that takes an optional value. This naming is unfortunate. It may help to think of these as default arguments rather than optional arguments.

A default parameter value is specified after the type in the function signature, with an equal sign (=) and then the expression. The expression is re-evaluated each time the function is called without a corresponding value. Default arguments are implicitly named so that the hash (indicating a named argument) is superfluous and will generate warnings.

In the `costOf` example, instead of passing the value of `costs` each time, it could be defined with a default parameter as follows:

```
> func costOf(#items:[String], costs:[String:Int] = costs) -> Int {
.    var cost = 0
.    for item in items {
.     if let cm = costs[item] {
.       cost += cm
.     }
.    }
.    return cost
. }
> costOf(items:shopping)
$R3: Int = 10
> costOf(items:shopping, costs:costs)
$R4: Int = 10
```

Note that in the first expression, the captured `costs` variable is bound when the function is defined. If `costs` is re-assigned at a later stage, then the function will not be updated.

Anonymous arguments

Swift requires that arguments with default values are named, as are arguments that are used in initializers for classes (which are covered in the *Classes in Swift* section in *Chapter 3, Creating an iOS Swift App*).

In some cases, this is unnecessary or unhelpful. To disable requiring a named argument for a parameter, the special value underscore (_) can be used:

```
> func costOf(items:[String], _ costs:[String:Int] = costs) -> Int {
.    var cost = 0
.    for item in items {
.        if let cm = costs[item] {
.            cost += cm
.        }
.    }
.    return cost
. }
> costOf(shopping)
$R0: Int = 10
> costOf(shopping,costs)
$R1: Int = 10
```

Multiple return values and arguments

So far, the examples of functions have all returned a single type. What happens if there is more than one return result from a function? In an object-oriented language, the answer is to return a class; however, Swift has tuples, which can be used to return multiple values. The type of a tuple is the type of its constituent parts:

```
> var pair = (1,2)
pair: (Int, Int) ...
```

This can be used to return multiple values from the function; instead of just returning one value, it is possible to return a tuple of values.

Swift also has in-out arguments, which will be seen in the *Handling Errors* section in *Chapter 6, Parsing Networked Data.*

Separately, it is also possible to take a variable number of arguments. A function can easily take an array of values with `[]`, but Swift provides a mechanism to allow calling with multiple arguments, using **variadic** functions. The last argument in a function signature can be variadic, which means that it has ellipses after the type. The value can then be used as an array in the function.

Taken together, these two features allow the creation of a `minmax` function, which returns both the minimum and maximum from a list of integers:

```
> func minmax(numbers:Int...) -> (Int,Int) {
.    var min = Int.max
.    var max = Int.min
.    for number in numbers {
.     if number < min {
.      min = number
.     }
.     if number > max {
.      max = number
.     }
.    }
.    return(min,max)
. }
> minmax(1,2,3,4)
$R0: (Int, Int) = {
   0 = 1
   1 = 4
}
```

The `numbers:Int...` indicates that a variable number of arguments can be passed into the function. Inside the function, it is processed as an ordinary array; in this case, iterating through using a `for...in` loop.

The `Int.max` constant represents the largest `Int` value, and `Int.min` is a constant representing the smallest `Int` value. Similar constants exist for specific integral types, such as `UInt8.max` and `Int64.min`.

What if no arguments are passed in? If run on a 64 bit system, then the output will be as follows:

```
> minmax()
$R1: (Int, Int) = {
  0 = 9223372036854775807
  1 = -9223372036854775808
}
```

This may not make sense for a `minmax` function. Instead of returning an error value or a default value, the type system can be used. By making the tuple optional, it is possible to return a `nil` value if it doesn't exist, or a tuple if it does:

```
> func minmax(numbers:Int...) -> (Int,Int)? {
.    var min = Int.max
.    var max = Int.min
.    if numbers.count == 0 {
.        return nil
.    } else {
.      for number in numbers {
.        if number < min {
.          min = number
.        }
.        if number > max {
.          max = number
.        }
.      }
.      return(min,max)
.  }
.  }
> minmax()
$R2: (Int, Int)? = nil
> mimmax(1,2,3,4)
```

```
$R3: (Int, Int)? = (0 = 1, 1 = 3)
> var (minimum,maximum) = minmax(1,2,3,4)!
minimum: Int = 1
maximum: Int = 4
```

Returning an optional value allows the caller to determine what should happen in cases where the maximum and minimum values are not present.

> If a function does not always have a valid return value, use an optional type to encode that possibility into the type system.

Returning structured values

A tuple is an ordered set of data. The entries in the tuple are ordered, but it can quickly become unclear as to what data is stored, particularly if they are of the same type. In the `minmax` tuple, it is unclear which value is the minimum and which is the maximum, and this can lead to subtle programming errors later on.

A structure is like a tuple, but with named values. This allows members to be accessed by name instead of by position, leading to fewer errors and greater transparency. Named values can be added to tuples as well. In essence, tuples with named values are anonymous structures.

> Structs are passed in a copy-by-value manner, like tuples. If two variables are assigned the same struct or tuple, then changes to one do not affect the value of another.

A **struct** is defined with the keyword `struct` and has variables or values in the body:

```
> struct MinMax {
.    var min:Int
.    var max:Int
. }
```

This defines a `MinMax` type, which can be used in place of any of the types seen so far. It can be used in the `minmax` function to return a `struct` instead of a tuple:

```
> func minmax(numbers:Int…) -> MinMax? {
.   var minmax = MinMax(min:Int.max, max:Int.min)
.   if numbers.count == 0 {
.     return nil
.   } else {
.     for number in numbers {
.       if number < minmax.min {
.         minmax.min = number
.       }
.       if number > minmax.max {
.         minmax.max = number
.       }
.     }
.     return minmax
.   }
. }
```

The `struct` is initialized with a type constructor; if `MinMax()` is used, then the default values for each of the structure members are used (based on the structure definition), but these defaults can be overridden explicitly if desired, with `MinMax(min:-10,max:11)`. For example, if the `MinMax` struct is defined as `struct MinMax { var min:Int = Int.max; var max:Int = Int.min }`, then `MinMax()` would return a structure with the appropriate maximum and minimum values filled in.

 When a structure is initialized, all the fields must be assigned. They can be passed in as named arguments in the initializer, or specified in the structure definition.

Swift also has classes; these are covered in the *Swift classes* section in the next chapter.

Command-line Swift

As Swift can be interpreted, it is possible to use it in shell scripts. By setting the interpreter to `swift` with a **hashbang**, the script can be executed without requiring a separate a compilation step. Alternatively, Swift scripts can be compiled to a native executable that can be run without the overhead of an interpreter.

Interpreted Swift scripts

Save the following as `hello.swift`:

```
#!/usr/bin/env xcrun swift
println("Hello World")
```

After saving, make the file executable by running `chmod a+x hello.swift`. The program can then be run by typing `./hello.swift`, and the traditional greeting will be seen:

```
Hello World
```

Arguments can be passed in from the command line and interrogated in the process using the `Process` class through the `arguments` constant. As with other Unix commands, the first element (0) is the name of the process executable; the arguments passed on in the command line start from one (1).

The program can be terminated using the `exit` function; however, this is defined in the `Foundation` framework and so it needs to be imported in order to call this function. Modules in Swift correspond to Frameworks in Objective-C and give access to all functions defined as public API in the module. The syntax to import all elements from a module is `import` module, although it's also possible to import a single function using `import func module.functionName`.

A Swift program to print arguments in uppercase can be implemented as follows:

```
#!/usr/bin/env xcrun swift
import Foundation
let args = Process.arguments[1..<countElements(Process.arguments)]
for arg in args {
  println("\(arg.uppercaseString)")
}
exit(0)
```

Running this with `hello world` results in the following:

```
$ ./upper.swift hello world
HELLO
WORLD
```

Conventionally, the entry point to Swift programs is via a script called `main.swift`. If starting a Swift-based command-line application project in Xcode, a `main.swift` file will be created automatically. Scripts do not need to have a `.swift` extension. For instance, the previous example could be called `upper` and it would still work.

Compiled Swift scripts

While interpreted Swift scripts are useful for experimenting and writing, each time the script is started, it is interpreted using the Swift command-line tool and then executed. For simple scripts (such as converting arguments to upper case), this can be a large proportion of the script's execution time.

To compile a Swift script into a native executable, use the `swiftc` command with the `-o` output flag to specify a file to write to. This will then generate an executable that does exactly the same as the interpreted script, only much faster. The `time` command can be used to compare the running time of the interpreted and compiled versions:

```
$ time ./upper.swift hello world # Interpreted
HELLO
WORLD
real   0m0.145s
$ xcrun swiftc -o upper upper.swift     # Compile step
$ time ./upper hello world       # Compiled
HELLO
WORLD
real   0m0.012s
```

Of course, the numbers will vary and the initial step only happens once, but startup is very lightweight in Swift. The numbers mentioned earlier are not meant to be taken in magnitude but rather as relative to each other.

The compile step can also be used to link together many individual Swift files into one executable, which helps create a more organized project; Xcode will encourage having multiple Swift files as well.

Summary

The Swift interpreter is a great way of learning how to program in Swift. It allows expressions, statements, and functions to be created and tested along with a command line history that provides editing support.

The basic collection types of arrays and collections and the standard data types, such as strings, numbers, collection types, optional values, and structures were presented. Control flow and functions with positional, named, and variadic arguments, along with default values were also presented. Finally, the ability to write Swift scripts and run them from the command line was also demonstrated.

The next chapter will look at the other way of working with Swift code—through the Xcode playground.

2
Playing with Swift

Xcode ships with both a command line interpreter (covered in *Chapter 1*, *Exploring Swift*) and a graphical interface called **playground** that can be used to prototype and test Swift code snippets. Code typed into the playground is compiled and executed interactively, which permits a fluid style of development. In addition, the user interface can present a graphical view of variables as well as a timeline, which can show how loops are executed. Finally, playgrounds can mix and match code and documentation, leading to the possibility of providing example code as playgrounds and using playgrounds to learn how to use existing APIs and frameworks.

This chapter will present the following topics:

- How to create a playground
- Displaying values in the timeline
- Presenting objects with Quick Look
- Running asynchronous code
- Using playground live documentation
- Generating playgrounds with Markdown and AsciiDoc
- Limitations of playgrounds

Getting started with playgrounds

When Xcode is started, a welcome screen is shown with various options, including the ability to create a playground. Playgrounds can also be created from the **File | New | Playground** menu.

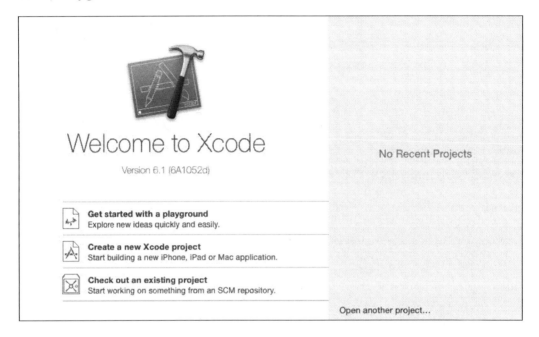

Creating a playground

Using either the Xcode welcome screen (which can be opened by navigating to **Window | Welcome to Xcode**) or navigating to **File | New | Playground**, create MyPlayground in a suitable location targeting iOS. Creating the playground on the Desktop will allow easy access to test Swift code, but it can be located anywhere on the filesystem.

Playgrounds can be targeted either towards OS X applications or towards iOS applications. This can be configured when the playground is created, or by switching to the **Utilities** view by navigating to **View | Utilities | Show File Inspector** or pressing *Command + Option + 1* and changing the dropdown from OS X to iOS or vice versa.

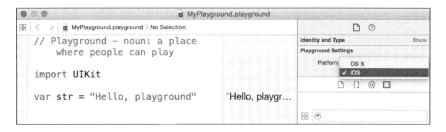

When initially created, the playground will have a code snippet that looks as follows:

```
// Playground - noun: a place where people can play
import UIKit
var str = "Hello, playground"
```

 Playgrounds targeting OS X will read `import Cocoa` **instead.**

On the right-hand side, a column will show the value of the code when each line is executed. In the previous example, the word **Hello, playgr...** is seen, which is the result of the string assignment. By grabbing the vertical divider between the Swift code and the output, the output can be resized to show the full text message:

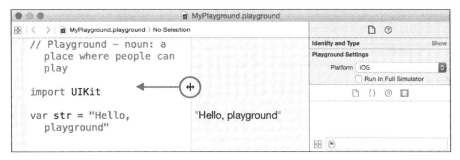

Alternatively, by moving the mouse over the right-hand side of the playground, the **Quick Look** icon (the eye symbol) will appear; if clicked on, a pop-up box will show the full details:

Viewing the console output

The console output can be viewed on the right-hand side by opening the **Assistant Editor**. This can be opened by pressing *Command + Option + Enter* or by navigating to **View | Assistant Editor | Show Assistant Editor**. This will show the result of any `println` statements executed in the code.

Add a simple `for` loop to the playground and show the **Assistant Editor**:

```
for i in 1...12 {
    println("I is \(i)")
}
```

The output is shown on the right-hand side:

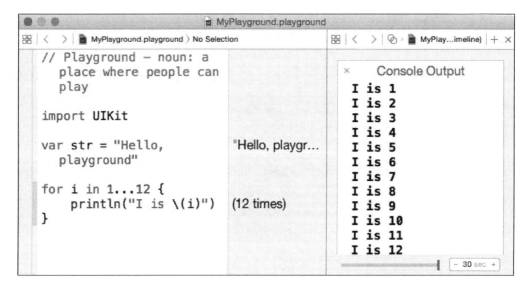

The assistant editor can be configured to be displayed in different locations, such as at the bottom, or stacked horizontally or vertically by navigating to the **View | Assistant Editor** menu.

Viewing the timeline

The timeline shows what other values are displayed as a result of executing the code. In the case of the print loop shown previously, the output was displayed as **Console Output** in the timeline. However, it is possible to use the playground to inspect the value of an expression on a line, without having to display it directly. In addition, results can be graphed to show how the values change over time.

Add another line above the `println` statement to calculate the result of executing an expression, `(i-6)*(i-7)`, and store it in a variable, `j`:

```
for i in 1...12 {
    var j = (i-7) * (i-6)
    println("I is \(i)")
}
```

On the line next to the variable definition, click on the add variable history symbol (**+**), which is in the right-hand column (visible when the mouse moves over that area). After it is clicked on, it will change to a (**o**) symbol and display the graph on the right-hand side. The same can be done for the `println` statement as well:

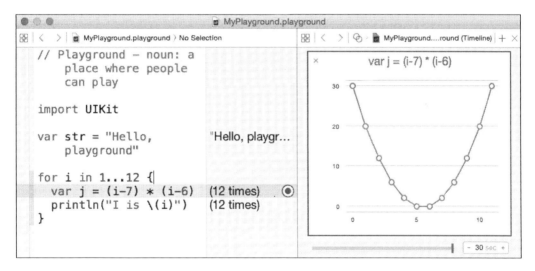

The slider at the bottom, indicated by the red tick mark, can be used to slide the vertical bar to see the exact value at certain points:

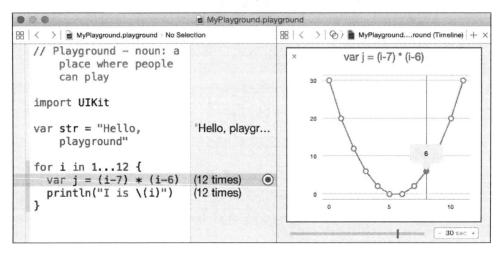

To show several values at once, use additional variables to hold the values and display them in the timeline as well:

```
for i in 1...12 {
    var j = (i-7) * (i-6)
    var k = i
    println("I is \(i)")
}
```

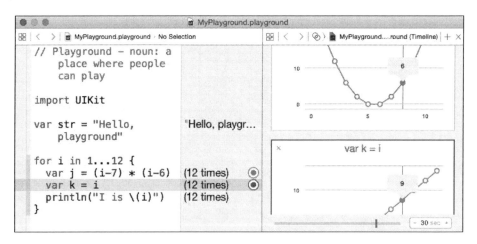

When the slider is dragged, both values will be shown at the same time.

Displaying objects with QuickLook

The playground timeline can display objects as well as numbers and simple strings. It is possible to load and view images in a playground using classes such as UIImage (or NSImage on OS X). These are known as **QuickLook supported objects**, and by default include:

- Strings (attributed and unattributed)
- Views
- Class and struct types (members are shown)
- Colors

 It is possible to build support for custom types in Swift, by implementing a debugQuickLookObject method that returns a graphical view of the data.

Showing colored labels

To show a colored label, a color needs to be obtained first. When building against iOS, this will be UIColor; but when building against OS X, it will be NSColor. The methods and types are largely equivalent between the two, but this chapter will focus on the iOS types.

A color can be acquired with an initializer or by using one of the predefined colors that are exposed in Swift using methods:

```
import UIKit // AppKit for OS X
let blue = UIColor.blueColor() // NSColor.blueColor() for OS X
```

The color can be used in a UILabel, which displays a text string in a particular size and color. The UILabel needs a size, which is represented by a CGRect, and can be defined with an x and y position along with a width and height. The x and y positions are not relevant for playgrounds and so can be left as zero:

```
let size = CGRect(x:0,y:0,width:200,height:100)
let label = UILabel(frame:size)// NSLabel for OS X
```

Finally, the text needs to be displayed in blue and with a larger font size:

```
label.text = str // from the first line of the code
label.textColor = blue
label.font = UIFont.systemFontOfSize(24) // NSFont for OS X
```

When the playground is run, the color and font are shown in the timeline and available for quick view. Even though the same `UILabel` instance is being shown, the timeline and the QuickLook values show a snapshot of the state of the object at each point, making it easy to see what has happened between changes.

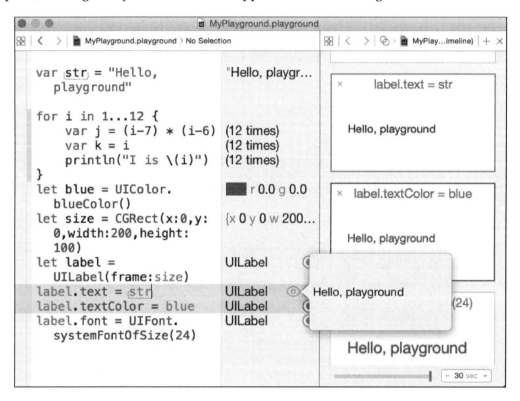

Showing images

Images can be created and loaded into a playground using the `UIImage` constructor (or `NSImage` on OS X). Both take a `named` argument, which is used to find an image with the given name from the playground's `Resources` folder.

To download a logo, open `Terminal.app` and run the following commands:

```
$ mkdir MyPlayground.playground/Resources
```

```
$ curl http://alblue.bandlem.com/images/AlexHeadshotLeft.png >
MyPlayground.playground/Resources/logo.png
```

An image can now be loaded in Swift with:

```
let logo = UIImage(named:"logo")
```

 The location of the `Resources` associated with a playground can be seen in the **File Inspector** utilities view, which can be opened by pressing *Command + Option + 1*.

The loaded image can be displayed using QuickLook or by adding it to the value history:

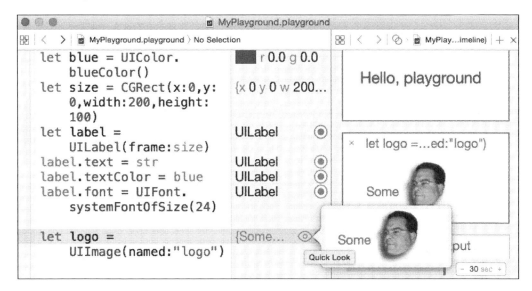

 It is possible to use a URL to acquire an image by creating an NSURL with `NSURL(string:"http://...")`, then loading the contents of the URL with `NSData(contentsOfURL:)`, and finally using `UIImage(data:)` to convert it to an image. However, as Swift will keep re-executing the code over and over again, the URL will be hit multiple times in a single debugging session without caching. It is recommended that `NSData(contentsOfURL:)` and similar networking classes be avoided in playgrounds.

Advanced techniques

The playground has its own framework, XCPlayground, which can be used to perform certain tasks. For example, individual values can be captured during loops for later analysis. It also permits asynchronous code to continue to execute once the playground has finished running.

Capturing values explicitly

It is possible to explicitly add values to the timeline by importing the XCPlayground framework and calling XCPCaptureValue with a value that should be displayed in the timeline. This takes an identifier, which is used both as the title and for group-related data values in the same series. When the value history button is selected, it essentially inserts a call to XCPCaptureValue with the value of the expression as the identifier.

For example, to add the logo to the timeline automatically:

```
import XCPlayground
XCPCaptureValue("logo",logo)
```

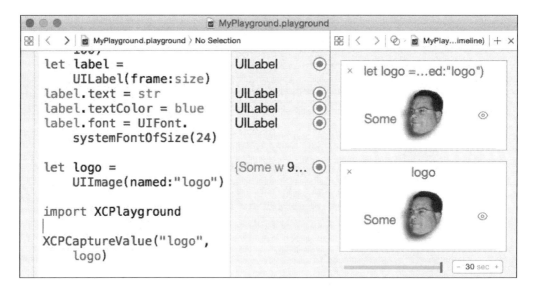

It is possible to use an identifier to group the data that is being shown in a loop with the identifier representing categories of the values. For example, to display a list of all even and odd numbers between 1 and 6, the following code could be used:

```
for n in 1...6 {
  if n % 2 == 0 {
    XCPCaptureValue("even",n)
    XCPCaptureValue("odd",0)
  } else {
    XCPCaptureValue("odd",n)
    XCPCaptureValue("even",0)
  }
}
```

The result, when executed, will look as follows:

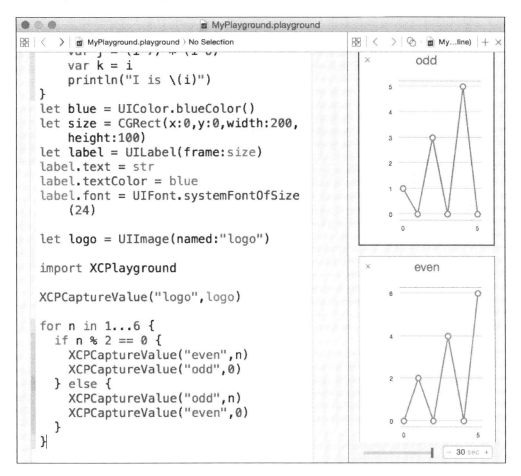

Running asynchronous code

By default, when the execution hits the bottom of the playground, the execution stops. In most cases, this is desirable, but when asynchronous code is involved, execution might need to run even if the main code has finished executing. This might be the case if networking data is involved or if there are multiple tasks whose results need to be synchronized.

For example, wrapping the previous even/odd split in an asynchronous call will result in no data being displayed:

```
dispatch_async(dispatch_get_main_queue()) {
  for n in 1...6 {
    // as before
  }
}
```

This uses one of Swift's language features: the `dispatch_async` method is actually a two-argument method that takes a queue and a block type. However, if the last argument is a block type, then it can be represented as a trailing closure rather than an argument.

To allow the playground to continue executing after reaching the bottom, add the following call:

```
XCPSetExecutionShouldContinueIndefinitely()
```

Although this suggests that the execution will run forever, it is limited to 30 seconds of runtime, or whatever is the value displayed at the bottom-right corner of the screen. This timeout can be changed by typing in a new value or using the + and – buttons to increase/decrease time by one second.

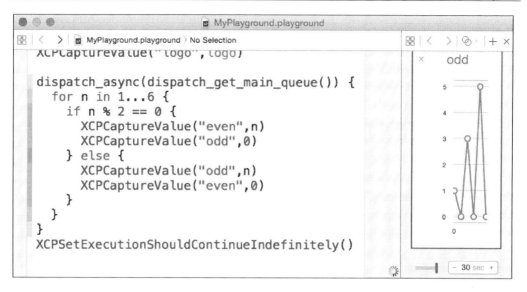

Playgrounds and documentation

Playgrounds can contain a mix of code and documentation. This allows a set of code samples and explanations to be mixed in with the playground itself. Although there is no way of using Xcode to add sections in the UI at present, the playground itself is an XML file that can be edited using an external text editor such as TextEdit.app.

Learning with playgrounds

As playgrounds can contain a mixture of code and documentation, it makes them an ideal format for viewing annotated code snippets. In fact, Apple's *Swift Tour* book can be opened as a playground file.

Xcode documentation can be searched by navigating to the **Help | Documentation and API Reference** menu, or by pressing *Command + Shift + 0*. In the search field that is presented, type `Swift Tour` and then select the first result. The Swift Tour book should be presented in Xcode's help system:

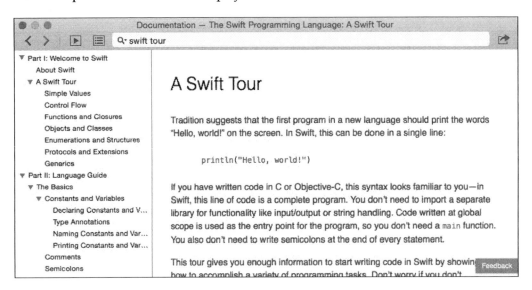

A link to download and open the documentation as a playground is given in the first section; if this is downloaded, it can be opened in Xcode as a standalone playground. This provides the same information, but allows the code examples to be dynamic and show the results in the window:

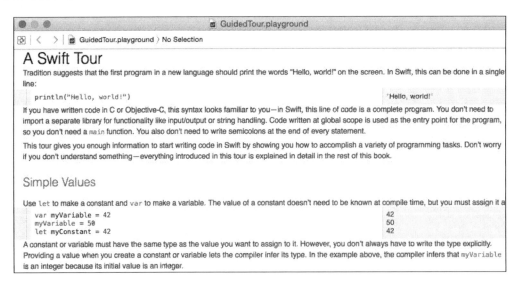

A key advantage of learning through playground-based documentation is that the code can be experimented with. In the **Simple Values** section of the documentation, where `myVariable` is assigned, the right-hand side of the playground shows the values. If the literal numbers are changed, the new values will be recalculated and shown on the right-hand side.

Some examples are presented solely in playground form; for example, the Balloons demo, which was used in the introduction of Swift in the WWDC 2014 keynote, is downloadable as a playground from `https://developer.apple.com/swift/resources/`.

> Note that the Balloons playground requires OS X 10.10 and Xcode 6.1 to run.

Understanding the playground format

A playground is an OS X **bundle**, which means that it is a directory that looks like a single file. If a playground is selected either in `TextEdit.app` or in `Finder`, then it looks like a regular file:

Under the covers, it is actually a directory:

```
$ ls -F
MyPlayground.playground/
```

Inside the directory, there are a number of files:

```
$ ls -1 MyPlayground.playground/*
MyPlayground.playground/Resources
MyPlayground.playground/contents.xcplayground
MyPlayground.playground/section-1.swift
MyPlayground.playground/timeline.xctimeline
```

The files are as follows:

- The `Resources` directory, which was created earlier to hold the logo image
- The `contents.xcplayground` file, which is an XML table of contents of the files that make up the playground
- The `section-1.swift` file, which is the Swift file created by default when a new playground is created, and contains the code that is typed in for any new playground content
- The `timeline.xctimeline` file, which is an automatically generated file containing timestamps of execution, which the runtime generates when executing a Swift file and the timeline is open

The table of contents file defines which runtime environment is being targeted (for example, iOS or OS X), a list of sections, and a reference to the timeline file:

```
<playground version='3.0' sdk='iphonesimulator'>
  <sections>
    <code source-file-name='section-1.swift'/>
  </sections>
  <timeline fileName='timeline.xctimeline'/>
</playground>
```

This file can be edited to add new sections, provided that it is not open in Xcode at the same time.

> An Xcode playground directory is deleted and recreated whenever changes are made in Xcode. Any `Terminal.app` windows open in that directory will no longer show any files. As a result, using external tools and editing the files in place might result in changes being lost. In addition, if you are using ancient versions of control systems, such as SVN and CVS, you might find your version control metadata being wiped out between saves. Xcode ships with the industry standard Git version control system, which should be preferred instead.

Adding a new documentation section

To add a new documentation section, ensure that the playground is not open in Xcode and then edit the `contents.xcplayground` file. The file itself can be opened by right-clicking on the playground in Finder and choosing **Show Package Contents**:

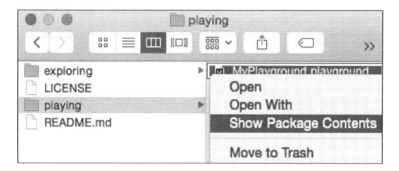

This will open up a new Finder window, with the contents displayed as a top-level set of elements. The individual files can then be opened for editing by right-clicking on the `contents.xcplayground` file, choosing **Open With | Other...**, and selecting an application, such as `TextEdit.app`.

Alternatively, the file can be edited from the command line using an editor such as `pico`, `vi`, or `emacs`.

Although there are few technology debates more contentious than whether `vi` or `emacs` is better, the recommended advice is to learn how to be productive in at least one of them. Like learning to touch-type, being productive in a command-line editor is something that will pay dividends in the future if the initial learning challenge can be overcome. For those who don't have time, `pico` (also known as `nano`) can be a useful tool in command-line situations, and the on-screen help makes it easier to learn to use. Note that the carat symbol (^) means control, so **^X** means *Control + X*.

To add a new documentation section, create a directory called `Documentation`, and inside it, create a file called `hello.html`. The HTML file is an HTML5 document, with a declaration and a body. A minimal file looks like:

```
<!DOCTYPE html>
<html>
  <body>
    <h1>Welcome to Swift Playground</h1>
  </body>
</html>
```

The content needs to be added to the table of contents (`contents.xcplayground`) in order to display it in the playground itself, by adding a `documentation` element under the `sections` element:

```
<playground version='3.0' sdk='iphonesimulator'>
  <sections>
    <code source-file-name='section-1.swift'/>
    <documentation relative-path='hello.html'/>
  </sections>
  <timeline fileName='timeline.xctimeline'/>
</playground>
```

The `relative-path` attribute is relative to the `Documentation` directory.

 All content in the `Documentation` directory is copied between saves in the timeline and can be used to store other text content such as CSS files. Binary content, including images, should be stored in the `Resources` directory.

When viewed as a playground, the content will be shown in the same window as the documentation:

If the content is truncated in the window, then a horizontal rule can be added at the bottom with <hr/>, or the documentation can be styled, as shown in the next section.

Styling the documentation

As the documentation is written in HTML, it is possible to style it using CSS. For example, the background of the documentation is transparent, which results in the text overlapping both the margins as well as the output.

To add a style sheet to the documentation, create a file called stylesheet.css in the Documentation directory and add the following content:

```
body {
   background-color: white
}
```

To add the style sheet to the HTML file, add a style sheet link reference to the head element in hello.html:

```
<head>
  <link rel="stylesheet" type="text/css" href="stylesheet.css"/>
</head>
```

Now when the playground is opened, the text will have a solid white background and will not be obscured by the margins:

```
        } else {
            XCPCaptureValue("odd",n)
            XCPCaptureValue("even",0)
        }
    }
}
XCPSetExecutionShouldContinueIndefinitely()
```

Welcome to Swift Playground

Adding resources to a playground

Images and other resources can also be added to a playground. Resources need to be added to a directory called `Resources`, which is copied as is between different versions of the playground.

To add an image to the document, create a `Resources` folder and then insert an image. For example, earlier in this chapter, an image was downloaded by using the following commands:

```
$ mkdir MyPlayground.playground/Resources
$ curl http://alblue.bandlem.com/images/AlexHeadshotLeft.png >
MyPlayground.playground/Resources/logo.png
```

The image can then be referred to in the documentation using an `img` tag and a relative path from the `Documentation` directory:

```
<img src="../Resources/logo.png" alt="Logo"/>
```

Other supported resources (such as JPEG and GIF) can be added to the `Resources` folder as well. It is also possible to add other content (such as a ZIP file of examples) to the `Resources` folder and provide hyperlinks from the documentation to the resource files.

```
<a href="../Resources/AlexBlewitt.vcf">Download contact card</a>
```

Additional entries in the header

The previous example showed the minimum amount of content required for playground documentation. However, there are other `meta` elements that can be added to the document that have specific purposes and which might be found in other playground examples on the internet. Here is a more comprehensive example of using `meta` elements:

```
<!DOCTYPE html>
<html lang="en">
  <head>
    <meta charset="utf-8"/>
    <link rel="stylesheet" type="text/css" href="stylesheet.css"/>
    <title>Welcome to Swift Playground</title>
    <meta name="xcode-display" content="render"/>
    <meta name="apple-mobile-web-app-capable" content="yes"/>
    <meta name="viewport" content="width=device-width,maximum-
scale=1.0"/>
```

```
    </head>
    <body>...</body>
</html>
```

In this example, the document is declared as being written in English (`lang="en"` on the `html` element) and in the UTF-8 character set.

> The `<meta charset="utf-8"/>` should always be the first element in the HTML `head` section, and the UTF-8 encoding should always be preferred for writing documents. If this is missed, it will default to a different encoding, such as ISO-8859-1, which can lead to strange characters appearing. Always use UTF-8 for writing HTML documents.

The `link` and `title` are standard HTML elements that associate the style sheet (from before) and the title of the document. The title is not displayed in Xcode, but it can be shown if the HTML document is opened in a browser instead. As the documentation is reusable between playgrounds and the web, it makes sense to give it a sensible title.

> The `link` should be the second element after the `charset` definition. In fact, all externally linked resources—such as style sheets and scripts—should occur near the top of the document. This allows the HTML parser to initiate the download of external resources as soon as possible. This also includes the HTML5 `prefetch` link type, which is not supported in Safari or playground at the time of writing.

The `meta` tags are instructions to Safari to render it in different ways (Safari is the web engine that is used to present the documentation content in playground). Safari-specific `meta` tags are described at `https://developer.apple.com/library/safari/documentation/AppleApplications/Reference/SafariHTMLRef/Articles/MetaTags.html` and include the following:

- The `xcode-display=render` meta tag, which indicates that Xcode should show the content of the document instead of the HTML source code when opening in Xcode

- The `apple-mobile-web-app-capable=yes` meta tag, which indicates that Safari should show this fullscreen if necessary when running on a mobile device

- The `viewport=width=device-width,maximum-scale=1.0` meta tag, which allows the document body to be resized to fit the user's viewable area without scaling

Generating playgrounds automatically

The format of the playground files are well known, and several utilities have been created to generate playgrounds from documentation formats, such as Markdown or AsciiDoc. These are text-based documentation formats that provide a standard means to generate output documents, particularly HTML-based ones.

Markdown

Markdown (a word play on markup) was created to provide a standard syntax to generate web page documentation with links and references in a plain text format. More information about Markdown can be found at the home page (`http://daringfireball.net/projects/markdown/`), and more about the standardization of **Markdown** into **CommonMark** (used by StackOverflow, GitHub, Reddit, and others) can be found at `http://commonmark.org`.

Embedding code in documentation is fairly common in Markdown. The file is treated as a top-level document, with sections to separate out the documentation and the code blocks. In CommonMark, these are separated with back ticks (```), often with the name of the language to add different script rendering types:

```
## Markdown Example ##
This is an example CommonMark document.

Blank lines separate paragraphs. Code blocks are introduced with three
back-ticks and closed with back-ticks:

```swift
println("Welcome to Swift")
```

Other text and other blocks can follow below.
```

The most popular tool for converting Markdown/CommonMark documents into playgrounds (at the time of writing) is Jason Sandmeyer's **swift-playground-builder** at `https://github.com/jas/swift-playground-builder/`. The tool uses Node to execute JavaScript and can be installed using the `npm install -g swift-playground-builder` command. Both Node and npm can be installed from `http://nodejs.org`.

Once installed, documents can be translated using `playground --platform ios --destination outdir --stylesheet stylesheet.css`. If code samples should not be editable, then the `--no-refresh` argument should be added.

AsciiDoc

AsciiDoc is similar in intent to Markdown, except that it can render to more backends than just HTML5. AsciiDoc is growing in popularity for documenting code, primarily because the standard is much more well defined than Markdown is. The de facto standard translation tool for AsciiDoc is written in Ruby and can be installed using the `sudo gem install asciidoctor` command.

Code blocks in AsciiDoc are represented by a `[source]` block. For Swift, this will be `[source, swift]`. The block starts and ends with two hyphens (`--`):

```
.AsciiDoc Example
This is an example AsciiDoc document.

Blank lines separate paragraphs. Code blocks are introduced with a
source block and two hyphens:

[source, swift]
--
println("Welcome to Swift")
--
```

Other text and other code blocks can follow below `--`.

AsciiDoc files typically use the `ad` extension, and the **ad2play** tool can be installed from James Carlson's repository at `https://github.com/jxxcarlson/ad2play`. Saving the preceding example as `example.ad` and running `ad2play example.ad` will result in the generation of the `example.playground` file.

More information about AsciiDoc, including the syntax and backend, can be found at the AsciiDoc home page at `http://www.methods.co.nz/asciidoc/` or on the Asciidoctor home page at `http://asciidoctor.org`.

Limitations of playgrounds

Although playgrounds can be very powerful for interacting with code, there are some limitations that are worth being aware of. There is no debugging support in the playground. It is not possible to add a breakpoint and use the debugger and find out what the values are. Given that the UI allows tracking values—and that it's very easy to add new lines with just the value to be tracked—this is not much of a hardship. Other limitations of playgrounds include:

- Only the simulator can be used for the execution of iOS-based playgrounds. This prevents the use of hardware-specific features that might only be present on a device.

- The performance of playground scripts is mainly driven based on how many lines are executed and how much output is saved by the debugger. It should not be used to test the performance of performance-sensitive code.

- Although the playground is well suited to present user interface components, it cannot be used for user input.

- Anything requiring entitlements (such as in-app purchases or access to iCloud) is not possible in playground at the time of writing.

 Note that while earlier releases of playground did not support custom frameworks, Xcode 6.1 permits frameworks to be loaded into playground, provided that the framework is built and marked as `public` and that it is in the same workspace as the playground.

Summary

This chapter presented playgrounds, an innovative way of running Swift code with graphical representations of values and introspection of running code. Both expressions and the timeline were presented as a way of showing the state of the program at any time, as well as graphically inspecting objects using QuickLook. The XCPlayground framework can also be used to record specific values and allow asynchronous code to be executed.

Being able to mix code and documentation into the same playground is also a great way of showing what functions exist, and how to create self-documenting playgrounds was presented. In addition, tools for the creation of such playgrounds using either AsciiDoc or Markdown (CommonMark) were introduced.

The next chapter will look at how to create an iOS application with Swift.

Creating an iOS Swift App 3

With the release of Xcode 6 in 2014, it is possible to build Swift applications for iOS and OS X and submit them to the App Store for publication. This chapter will present both a single view application and a master-detail application, and use these to explain the concepts behind iOS applications as well as introduce classes in Swift.

This chapter will present the following topics:

- How iOS applications are structured
- Single view iOS applications
- Creating classes in Swift
- Protocols and enums in Swift
- Using XCTest to test Swift code
- Master-detail iOS applications
- The `AppDelegate` and `ViewController` classes

Understanding iOS applications

An iOS application is a compiled executable, along with a set of supporting files in a bundle. The application bundle is packaged into an archive file for installing onto a device or uploading to the App Store.

Xcode can be used to run iOS applications in a simulator, but running an application on a device requires a developer signing key, which is included as part of the iOS developer program at `https://developer.apple.com`.

Most iOS applications to date have been written in Objective-C, a crossover between C and Smalltalk. With the advent of Swift, it is likely that many developers will move at least parts of their applications to Swift for performance and maintenance reasons. Although Objective-C is likely to be around for a while, it is clear that Swift is the future of iOS development, and probably OS X as well.

Applications contain a number of different types of files, which are used both at compile time and also at runtime. These files include:

- The `Info.plist` file, which contains information about which languages the application is localized for, what the identity of the application is, and the configuration requirements, such as the supported interface types (iPad, iPhone, and Universal) and orientations (Portrait, Upside Down, Landscape Left, and Landscape Right)
- Zero or more **interface builder** files with a `.xib` extension, which contain user interface screens (which supersedes the previous `.nib` files)
- Zero or more **image asset** files with a `.xcassets` extension, which store groups of related icons at different sizes, such as the application icon or graphics for display on screen (which supersedes the previous `.icns` files)
- Zero or more **storyboard** files with a `.storyboard` extension, which are used to coordinate between different screens in an application
- One or more `.swift` files that contain application code

Creating a single view iOS application

A single view iOS application is one where the application is presented in a single screen, without any transitions or other views. This section will show how to create an application that uses a single view without storyboards. (Storyboards are covered in *Chapter 4, Storyboard Applications with Swift and iOS*.)

When Xcode starts, it displays a welcome message that includes the ability to create a new project. This welcome message can be redisplayed at any time by navigating to **Window | Welcome to Xcode** or by pressing *Command + Shift + 1*.

Using the welcome dialog's **Create a new Xcode project** option, by navigating to **File | New | Project...**, or by pressing *Command + Shift + N*, create a new project and select **Single View Application** as the template, as shown in the following screenshot:

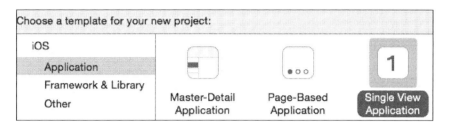

When the **Next** button is pressed, the new project dialog will ask for more details. The product name here is `SingleView` with appropriate values for **Organization Name** and **Identifier**. Ensure that the language selected is **Swift** and the device type is **Universal**:

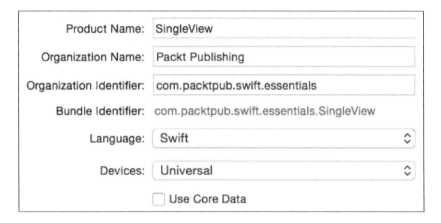

 The **Organization Identifier** is a reverse domain name representation of the organization, and the **Bundle Identifier** is the concatenation of the **Organization Identifier** with the **Product Name**. Publishing to the App Store requires that the **Organization Identifier** be owned by the publisher and is managed in the online developer center at `https://developer.apple.com/membercenter/`.

When **Next** is pressed, Xcode will ask where to save the project and whether a repository should be created. The selected location will be used to create the product directory, and an option to create a Git repository will be offered.

In 2014, Git became the most widely used version control system, surpassing all other distributed and centralized version control systems. It is foolish not to create a Git repository when creating a new Xcode project.

When **Create** is pressed, Xcode will create the project, set up template files, and then initialize the Git repository locally or on a shared server.

Press the triangular play button at the top-left of Xcode to launch the simulator:

If everything has been set up correctly, the simulator will start with a white screen and the time and battery shown at the top of the screen:

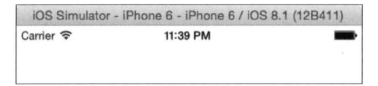

Removing the storyboard

The default template for a single view application includes a **storyboard**. This creates the view for the first (only) screen and performs some additional setup behind the scenes. To understand what happens, the storyboard will be removed and replaced with code instead.

 Most applications are built with one or more storyboards. It is being removed here for demonstration purposes only; see the next chapter, *Storyboards, Scenes, and Segues*, for more information on how to use storyboards.

The storyboard can be deleted by going to the project navigator, finding the Main.storyboard file, and pressing the *Delete* key or selecting **Delete** from the context-sensitive menu. When the confirmation dialog is shown, select the **Move to Trash** option to ensure that the file is deleted rather than just being removed from the list of files that Xcode knows about.

To see the project navigator, press *Command + 1* or navigate to **View | Navigators | Show Project Navigator**.

Once `Main.storyboard` has been deleted, it needs to be removed from `Info.plist` to prevent iOS from trying to open it at startup. Open `Info.plist` under the `Supporting Files` folder of `SingleView`. A set of key-value pairs will be shown; clicking on the **Main storyboard file base name** row will present the **(+)** and **(-)** options. Clicking on the delete icon **(-)** will remove the line.

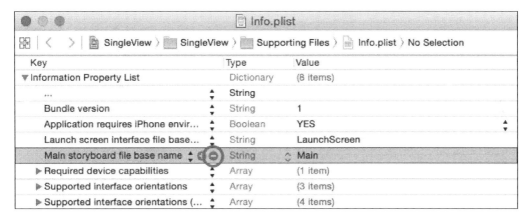

Now, when the application is started, a black screen will be shown.

 There are two `Info.plist` files created by Xcode's template; one file is used for the real application, while the other file is used for the test application that gets built when running tests. Testing is covered in the *Subclasses and testing in Swift* section later in this chapter.

Setting up the view controller

The **view controller** is responsible for setting up the view when it is activated. Typically, this is done through either the storyboard or the interface file. Since these have been removed, the window and the view controller need to be instantiated manually.

When an iOS application starts, `application:didFinishLaunchingWithOptions:` is called on `UIApplicationDelegate`. The optional `window` variable is initialized automatically when it is loaded from an interface file or a storyboard, but it needs to be explicitly initialized if the user interface is being implemented in code.

Implement the `application:didFinishLaunchingWithOptions:` method in the `AppDelegate` class as follows:

```
@UIApplicationMain
class AppDelegate: UIResponder, UIApplicationDelegate {
  var window: UIWindow?
  func application(application: UIApplication,
   didFinishLaunchingWithOptions launchOptions:
   [NSObject:AnyObject]?) -> Bool {
    window = UIWindow()
    window?.rootViewController = ViewController()
    window?.makeKeyAndVisible()
    return true
  }
}
```

 To open a class by name, press *Command* + *Shift* + *O* and type in the class name. Alternatively, **File** | **Open Quickly....** can be used instead

The final step is to create the view's content, which is typically done in the `viewDidLoad` method of the `ViewController` class. As an example user interface, `UILabel` will be created and added to the view. Each view controller has an associated `view` property, and child views can be added with the `addSubview` method. To make the view stand out, the background of the view will be changed to black and the text color will be changed to white:

```
class ViewController: UIViewController {
  override func viewDidLoad() {
    super.viewDidLoad()
    view.backgroundColor = UIColor.blackColor()
    var label = UILabel(frame:view.bounds)
    label.textColor = UIColor.whiteColor()
    label.textAlignment = .Center
    label.text = "Welcome to Swift"
    view.addSubview(label)
  }
}
```

This creates a label, which is sized to the full size of the screen, with a white text color and a centered text alignment. This displays **Welcome to Swift** on the screen.

Typically views will be implemented in their own class rather than being in-lined into the view controller. This allows the views to be reused in other controllers. This technique will be demonstrated in the next chapter.

When the screen is rotated, the label will be rotated off screen. Logic would need to be added in a real application to handle rotation changes in the view controller, such as `willRotateToInterfaceOrientation`, and to appropriately add rotations to the views using the `transform` property of the view. Usually, an interface builder file or storyboard would be used so that this is handled automatically.

Swift classes, protocols, and enums

Almost all Swift applications will be object oriented. *Chapter 1*, *Exploring Swift*, and *Chapter 2*, *Playing with Swift*, both demonstrated functional and procedural Swift code. Classes such as `Process` from the `CoreFoundation` framework, and `UIColor` and `UIImage` from the `UIKit` framework were used to demonstrate how classes can be used in applications. This section describes how to create classes, protocols, and enums in Swift.

Classes in Swift

A class is created in Swift using the `class` keyword and braces are used to enclose the class body. The body can contain variables called **properties** as well as functions called **methods**, which are collectively referred to as **members**. Instance members are unique to each instance, while class members are shared between all instances of that class.

Classes are typically defined in a file named for the class; so a `GitHubRepository` class can be defined in the `GitHubRepository.swift` file. A new Swift file can be created by navigating to **File** | **New** | **File...** and selecting the **Swift** option under **iOS**:

```
class GitHubRepository {
  var id:UInt64 = 0
  var name:String = ""
  func detailsURL() -> String {
    return "https://api.github.com/repositories/\(id)"
  }
}
```

This class can be instantiated and used as follows:

```
var repo = GitHubRepository()
repo.id = 1
repo.name = "Grit"
repo.detailsURL() // returns https://api.github.com/repositories/1
```

It is possible to create class members, which are the same for all instances of a class. In the GitHubRepository class, the api URL is likely to remain the same for all invocations, so it can be refactored into a class property:

```
class GitHubRepository {
  // does not work in Swift 1.0 or 1.1
  class let api = "https://api.github.com"
  ...
  func detailsURL() -> String {
    return "\(api)/repositories/\(id)"
  }
}
```

Now, if the api URL needs to be changed (for example, to support mock testing or to support an in-house GitHub Enterprise server), there is a single place to change it.

 In Xcode 6.1 with Swift 1.1, an error message the **class variables are not yet supported** may be seen.

To use class variables in Swift 1.1, a different approach must be used. It is possible to define **computed properties**, which are not stored but are calculated on demand. These have a **getter** (also known as an accessor) and optionally a **setter** (also known as a mutator). The previous example can be rewritten as:

```
class GitHubRepository {
  class var api:String {
    get {
      return "https://api.github.com"
    }
  }
  func detailsURL() -> String {
    return "\(GitHubRepository.api)/repositories/\(id)"
  }
}
```

Although this is logically a read-only constant (there is no associated `set` block), it is not possible to define `let` constants with accessors.

To refer to a class variable, use the type name—which in this case is `GitHubRepository`. When the expression `GitHubRepository.api` is evaluated, the body of the getter is called.

Subclasses and testing in Swift

A simple Swift class with no explicit parent is known as a **base class**. However, classes in Swift frequently **inherit** from another class by specifying a superclass. The syntax for this is `class SubClass:SuperClass{...}`.

Tests in Swift are written using the **XCTest** framework, which is included by default in Xcode templates. This allows an application to have tests written and then executed in place to confirm that no bugs have been introduced.

 XCTest replaces the previous testing framework OCUnit.

The `XCTest` framework has a base class called `XCTestCase` that all tests inherit from. Methods beginning with `test` (and that take no arguments) in the test case class are invoked automatically when the tests are run. Test code can indicate success or failure by calling the `XCTAssert*` functions, such as `XCTAssertEquals` and `XCTAssertGreaterThan`.

Tests for the `GitHubRepository` class conventionally exist in a corresponding `GitHubRepositoryTest` class, which will be a subclass of `XCTestCase`. It can be implemented as:

```
import XCTest
class GitHubRepositoryTest: XCTestCase {
  func testRepository() {
    var repo = GitHubRepository()
    repo.id = 1
    repo.name = "Grit"
    XCTAssertEqual(
      repo.detailsURL(),
      "https://api.github.com/repositories/1",
      "Repository details"
    )
  }
}
```

Make sure that the `GitHubRepositoryTest` class is added to the test target by selecting the file and pressing *Command + Option + 1* to show the File Inspector. The checkbox next to the test target should be selected. Tests should never be added to the main target. The `GitHubRepository` class should be added to both targets:

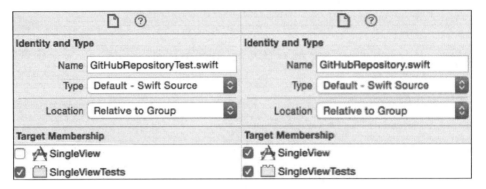

When the tests are run by pressing *Command + U* or by navigating to **Product | Test**, the results of the test will be shown. Changing either the implementation or the expected test result will demonstrate whether the test is being executed correctly.

Always check whether a failing test causes the build to fail; this will confirm that the test is actually being run. For example, in the `GitHubRepositoryTest` class, modify the URL to remove `https` from the front and check whether a test failure is shown. There is nothing more useless than a correctly implemented test that never runs.

Protocols in Swift

A **protocol** is similar to an interface in other languages; it is a named type that has method signatures but no method implementations. Classes can implement zero or more protocols; when they do, they are said to **adopt** or **conform** to the protocol. A protocol might have a number of methods that are either **required** (the default) or **optional** (marked with the `optional` keyword).

Optional protocol methods are only supported when the protocol is marked with the `@objc` attribute. This declares that the class will be backed by an `NSObject` class for interoperability with Objective-C. Pure Swift protocols cannot have optional methods.

The syntax for defining a protocol looks like:

```
protocol GitHubDetails {
  func detailsURL() -> String
  // protocol needs @objc if using optional protocols
  // optional doNotNeedToImplement()
}
```

Note that protocols cannot have functions with default arguments. Protocols can be used against the `struct`, `class`, and `enum` types unless the `@objc` class attribute is used, in which case they can only be used against Objective-C classes or enums.

Classes conform to protocols by listing the protocol names after the class name, similar to a superclass.

When a class has both a superclass and one or more protocols, the superclass should be listed first.

```
class GitHubRepository: GitHubDetails {
  func detailsURL() -> String {
    // implementation as before
  }
}
```

The `GitHubDetails` protocol can be used as a type in the same places as an existing Swift type, such as a variable type, method return type, or argument type.

Protocols are widely used in Swift to allow callbacks from frameworks that would otherwise not know about specific callback handlers. If a superclass was required instead, then a single class could not be used to implement multiple callbacks. Common protocols include `UIApplicationDelegate`, `Printable`, and `Comparable`.

Enums in Swift

The final concept to understand in Swift is **enumeration**, or **enum** for short. An enum is a closed set of values, such as `North`, `East`, `South`, and `West` or `Up` and `Down`.

An enumeration is defined using the `enum` keyword followed by a type name and a block, which contains `case` keywords followed by comma-separated values:

```
enum Suit {
    case Clubs, Diamonds, Hearts // many on one line
    case Spades // or each on separate lines
}
```

Unlike C, enumerated values do not have a specific type by default, so they cannot be converted to and from an integer value. Enumerations can be defined with **raw values** that allow conversion to and from integer values. Enum values are assigned to variables using the type name and the enum name:

```
var suit:Suit = Suit.Clubs
```

However, if the type of the expression is known, then the type prefix does not need to be explicitly specified. So the following form is much more common in Swift code:

```
var suit:Suit = .Clubs
```

Raw values

For `enum` values that have specific meanings, it is possible to extend the `enum` from a different type, such as `Int`. These are known as **raw values**.

```
enum Rank: Int {
    case Two = 2, Three, Four, Five, Six, Seven, Eight, Nine, Ten
    case Jack, Queen, King, Ace
}
```

A raw value enum can be converted to and from its raw value with the `rawValue` property and the failable initializer `Rank(rawValue:)` as follows:

```
Rank.Two.rawValue == 2
Rank(rawValue:14)! == Rank.Ace
```

Note that the failable initializer returns an optional enum value, because the equivalent Rank might not exist. The expression Rank(rawValue:0) will return nil, for example.

Associated values

Enums can also have **associated values**, such as a value or case class in other languages. For example, a combination of a Suit and a Rank can be combined to form a Card:

```
enum Card {
  case Face(Rank, Suit)
  case Joker
}
```

Instances can be created by passing values into an enum initializer:

```
var aceOfSpades: Card = .Face(.Ace,.Spades)
var twoOfHearts: Card = .Face(.Two,.Hearts)
var theJoker: Card = .Joker
```

The values of an enum cannot be extracted (as they can with a struct), but the enum value can be accessed by pattern matching in a switch statement:

```
var card = aceOfSpades // or theJoker or twoOfHearts ...
switch card {
  case .Face(var rank, var suit):
    println("Got a face card \(rank) of \(suit)");
  case .Joker:
    println("Got the joker card")
}
```

The Swift compiler will ensure that the switch statement is exhaustive. Since the enum only contains these two types, no default block is needed. If another enum value is added to Card in the future, the compiler will report an error in this switch statement.

Creating a master-detail iOS application

Having covered how classes, protocols, and enums are defined in Swift, a more complex master-detail application can be created. A master-detail application is a specific type of iOS application that initially presents a table view, and when an individual element is selected, a secondary details view will show more information about the selected item.

Using the **Create a new Xcode project** option from the welcome screen, navigate to **File | New | Project...** or press *Command + Shift + N*, and select **Master-Detail Application** from the **iOS Application** category:

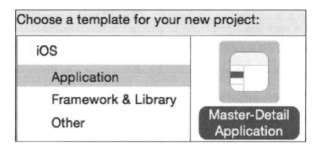

In the subsequent dialog, enter appropriate values for the project, such as the name (`MasterDetail`), the organizational identifier (typically based on the reverse DNS name), ensure that the **Language** drop-down reads **Swift** and that it is targeted for **Universal** devices.

When the project is created, an Xcode window will open, containing all the files created by the wizard itself, including the **MasterDetail.app** and **MasterDetailTests. xctest** products. The `MasterDetail.app` is a bundle that is executed by the simulator or a connected device, while the `MasterDetailTests.xctest` product is used to execute unit tests for the application's code.

The application can be launched by pressing the triangular play button on the top-left corner of Xcode or by pressing *Command + R*, which will run the application against the currently selected target.

After a brief compile and build cycle, the iOS Simulator will open with a master page that contains an empty table:

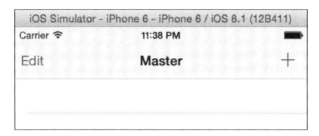

The default `MasterDetail` application can be used to add items to the list, by clicking on the add (+) button on the top-right corner of the screen. This will add a new timestamped entry to the list.

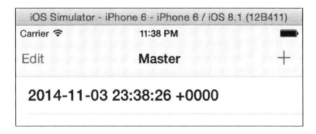

When this item is clicked, the screen will switch to the details view, which in this case presents the time in the center of the screen:

This kind of master-detail application is common in iOS applications to display a top-level list (such as a shopping list, a set of contacts, to-do notes, and so on) while allowing the user to tap to see the details.

There are three main classes in the master-detail application:

- `AppDelegate`: This class is defined in the `AppDelegate.swift` file, and is responsible for starting the application and setting up the initial state
- `MasterViewController`: This class is defined in the `MasterViewController.swift` file, and is used to manage the first (master) screen's content and interactions
- `DetailViewController`: This class is defined in the `DetailViewController.swift` file, and is used to manage the second (detail) screen's content

In order to understand what the classes do in more detail, the next three sections will present each one of them in turn.

 The code generated in this section was created from Xcode 6.1, so the templates might differ slightly if using a different version of Xcode. An exact copy of the corresponding code can be acquired from the Packt website or from the book's GitHub repository at `https://github.com/alblue/com.packtpub.swift.essentials/`.

The AppDelegate class

The `AppDelegate` class is the main entry point to the application. When a set of Swift source files are compiled, if the `main.swift` file exists, it is used as the entry point for the application by running that code. However, to simplify setting up an application for iOS, a special attribute `@UIApplicationMain` exists which will both synthesize the `main` method and set up the associated class as the application delegate.

The `AppDelegate` class for iOS extends the `UIResponder` class, which is the parent of all the UI content on iOS. It also adopts two protocols, `UIApplicationDelegate` and `UISplitViewControllerDelegate`, which are used to provide callbacks when certain events occur:

```
@UIApplicationMain
class AppDelegate: UIResponder, UIApplicationDelegate,
   UISplitViewControllerDelegate {
  var window: UIWindow?
  ...
}
```

On OS X, the AppDelegate class will be a subclass of NSApplication and will adopt the NSApplicationDelegate protocol.

The synthesized `main` function calls the `UIApplicationMain` method that reads the `Info.plist` file. If the `UILaunchStoryboardName` key exists and points to a suitable file (the `LaunchScreen.xib` interface file in this case), it will be shown as a splash screen before doing any further work. After the rest of the application has loaded, if the `UIMainStoryboardFile` key exists and points to a suitable file (the `Main.storyboard` file in this case), the storyboard is launched and the initial view controller is shown.

The storyboard has references to the `MasterViewController` and `DetailViewController` classes. The `window` variable is assigned to the storyboard's window.

Once the application has been loaded, the `application:didFinishLaunching WithOptions:` callback is called with a reference to the `UIApplication` instance and a dictionary of options that notifies how the application has been started:

```
func application(
 application: UIApplication,
 didFinishLaunchingWithOptions launchOptions:
  [NSObject: AnyObject]?) -> Bool {
  // Override point for customization after application launch.
  ...
}
```

In the sample `MasterDetail` application, the `application:didFinishLaunching WithOptions:` method acquires a reference to the `splitViewController` from the explicitly unwrapped optional `window`, and the `AppDelegate` is set as its delegate:

```
let splitViewController =
 self.window!.rootViewController as UISplitViewController
splitViewController.delegate = self
```

 The syntax `... as UISplitViewController` performs a type cast so that the generic `rootViewController` can be assigned to the more specific type; in this case, `UISplitViewController`.

Finally, the `navigationController` is acquired from the `splitViewController`, which stores an array of `viewControllers`. This allows the `DetailView` to show a button on the left-hand side to expand the details view, if necessary:

```
let navigationController = splitViewController.viewController
  [splitViewController.viewControllers.count-1]
  as UINavigationController
navigationController.topViewController
  .navigationItem.leftBarButtonItem =
  splitViewController.displayModeButtonItem()
```

The only difference this makes is when running on a wide-screen device, such as an iPhone 6 Plus or an iPad, where the views are shown side-by-side in landscape mode. This is a new feature in iOS 8 applications.

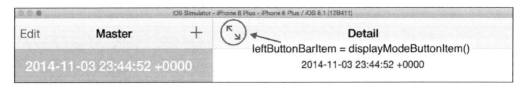

Otherwise, when the device is in portrait mode, it will be rendered as a standard back button:

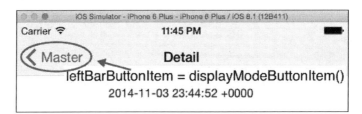

The method concludes with `return true` to let the OS know that the application opened successfully.

The MasterViewController class

The `MasterViewController` class is responsible for coordinating the data shown on the first screen (when the device is in portrait orientation) or the left-half of the screen (when a large device is in landscape orientation). This is rendered with a `UITableView`, and data is coordinated through the parent `UITableViewController` class:

```
class MasterViewController: UITableViewController {
  var objects = NSMutableArray()
  override func viewDidLoad() {...}
  func insertNewObject(sender: AnyObject) {...}
  ...
}
```

The `viewDidLoad` method is used to set up or initialize the view after it has loaded. In this case, a `UIBarButtonItem` is created so that the user can add new entries to the table. The `UIBarButtonItem` takes a `@selector` in Objective-C, and in Swift, is treated as a string literal convertible (so that `"insertNewObject:"` will result in a call to the `insertNewObject` method). Once created, the button is added to the navigation on the right-hand side, using the standard `.Add` type which will be rendered as a **+** sign on the screen:

```
override func viewDidLoad() {
  super.viewDidLoad()
  let addButton = UIBarButtonItem(
    barButtonSystemItem: .Add, target: self,
    action: "insertNewObject:")
  self.navigationItem.rightBarButtonItem = addButton
  self.navigationItem.leftBarButtonItem = self.editButtonItem()
}
```

The objects are `NSDate` values and are stored inside the class as an `NSMutableArray`. The `insertNewObject` method is called when the **+** button is pressed, and creates a new `NSDate` instance, which is then inserted into the array. The event `sender` is passed as an argument of the `AnyObject` type, which will be a reference to the `UIBarButtonItem` (although it is not needed or used here):

```
func insertNewObject(sender: AnyObject) {
  objects.insertObject(NSDate.date(), atIndex: 0)
  let indexPath = NSIndexPath(forRow: 0, inSection: 0)
  self.tableView.insertRowsAtIndexPaths(
    [indexPath], withRowAnimation: .Automatic)
}
```

The `UIBarButtonItem` class was created before blocks were available on iOS devices, so it uses the older Objective-C `@selector` mechanism. A future release of iOS might provide an alternative that takes a block, in which case Swift functions can be passed instead.

The parent class contains a reference to the `tableView`, which is automatically created by the storyboard. When an item is inserted, the `tableView` is notified that a new object is available. Standard `UITableViewController` methods are used to access the data from the array:

```
override func numberOfSectionsInTableView(
  tableView: UITableView) -> Int {
  return 1
}
override func tableView(tableView: UITableView,
  numberOfRowsInSection section: Int) -> Int {
  return objects.count
}
override func tableView(tableView: UITableView,
  cellForRowAtIndexPath indexPath: NSIndexPath) -> UITableViewCell{
  let cell = tableView.dequeueReusableCellWithIdentifier(
    "Cell", forIndexPath: indexPath) as UITableViewCell
  let object = objects[indexPath.row] as NSDate
  cell.textLabel?.text = object.description
  return cell
}
override func tableView(tableView: UITableView,
  canEditRowAtIndexPath indexPath: NSIndexPath) -> Bool {
  return true
}
```

The `numberOfSectionsInTableView` function returns 1 in this case, but a `tableView` can have multiple sections, for example, to permit a contacts application having a different section for A, B, C through Z. The `numberOfRowsInSection` method returns the number of elements in each section; in this case, since there is only one section, the number of objects in the array.

The reason why each method is called `tableView` and takes a `tableView` argument is a result of the Objective-C heritage of UIKit. The Objective-C convention combined the method name as the first named argument, so the original method was `[delegate tableView:UITableView, numberOfRowsInSection: NSInteger]`. As a result, the name of the first argument is reused as the name of the method in Swift.

The `cellForRowAtIndexPath` method is expected to return a `UITableViewCell` for an object. In this case, a cell is acquired from the `tableView` using the `dequeueReusableCellWithIdentifier` method (which caches cells as they go off screen to save object instantiation) and then the `textLabel` is populated with the object's `description` (which is a `String` representation of the object; in this case, the date).

This is enough to display elements in the table, but in order to permit editing (or just removal, as in the sample application), there are some additional protocol methods that are required:

```
override func tableView(tableView: UITableView,
  canEditRowAtIndexPath indexPath: NSIndexPath) -> Bool {
    return true
}
override func tableView(tableView: UITableView,
  commitEditingStyle editingStyle: UITableViewCellEditingStyle,
  forRowAtIndexPath indexPath: NSIndexPath) {
    if editingStyle == .Delete {
      objects.removeObjectAtIndex(indexPath.row)
      tableView.deleteRowsAtIndexPaths([indexPath],
        withRowAnimation: .Fade)
    }
}
```

The `canEditRowAtIndexPath` method returns `true` if the row is editable; if all the rows can be edited, then this will return `true` for all the values.

The `commitEditingStyle` method takes a table, a path, and a style which is an enumeration that indicates which operation occurred. In this case, `UITableViewCellEditingStyle.Delete` is passed in order to delete the item from both the underlying object array and also from the `tableView`. (The enumeration can be abbreviated to `.Delete` because the type of the `editingStyle` is known to be `UITableViewCellEditingStyle`.)

The DetailViewController class

The detail view is shown when an element is selected in the `MasterViewController`. The transition is managed by the storyboard controller; the views are connected with a **segue** (pronounced segway; the product of the same name based it on the word *segue* which is derived from the Italian word for *follows*).

To pass the selected item between controllers, a property exists in the DetailViewController class called detailItem. When the value is changed, additional code is run, which is implemented in a didSet property notification:

```
class DetailViewController: UIViewController {
  var detailItem: AnyObject? {
    didSet {
      self.configureView()
    }
  }
  ...
}
```

When the DetailViewController has the detailItem set, the configureView method will be invoked. The didSet body is run after the value has been changed, but before the setter returns to the caller. This is triggered by the segue in the MasterViewController:

```
class MasterViewController: UIViewController {
  ...
  override func prepareForSegue(
    segue: UIStoryboardSegue, sender: AnyObject?) {
    super.prepareForSegue(segue, sender: sender)
    if segue.identifier == "showDetail" {
      if let indexPath =
        self.tableView.indexPathForSelectedRow() {
        let object = objects[indexPath.row] as NSDate
        let controller = (segue.destinationViewController
          as UINavigationController)
          .topViewController as DetailViewController
        controller.detailItem = object
        controller.navigationItem.leftBarButtonItem =
          self.splitViewController?.displayModeButtonItem()
        controller.navigationItemleftItemsSupplementBackButton =
          true
      }
    }
  }
}
```

The `prepareForSegue` method is called when the user selects an item in the table. In this case, it grabs the selected row index from the table and uses this to acquire the selected date object. The navigation controller hierarchy is searched to acquire the `DetailViewController`, and once this has been obtained, the selected value is set with `controller.detailItem = object`, which triggers the update.

The label is ultimately displayed in the `DetailViewController` through the `configureView` method, which stamps the `description` of the object onto the `label` in the center:

```
class DetailViewController {
  ...
  @IBOutlet weak var detailDescriptionLabel: UILabel!
  function configureView() {
    if let detail: AnyObject = self.detailItem {
      if let label = self.detailDescriptionLabel {
        label.text = detail.description
      }
    }
  }
}
```

The `configureView` method is called both when the `detailItem` is changed and when the view is loaded for the first time. If the `detailItem` has not been set, then this has no effect.

The implementation introduces some new concepts, which are worth highlighting:

- The `@IBOutlet` attribute indicates that the property will be exposed in interface builder and can be wired up to the object instance. This will be covered in more detail in *Chapter 4, Storyboard Applications with Swift and iOS*, and in *Chapter 5, Creating Custom Views in Swift*.

- The `weak` attribute indicates that the property will not store a **strong** reference to the object; in other words, the detail view will not own the object but merely reference it. Generally, all `@IBOutlet` references should be declared as `weak` to avoid cyclic dependency references.

- The type is defined as `UILabel!`, which is an **implicitly unwrapped optional**. When accessed, it performs an explicit unwrapping of the optional value; otherwise the `@IBOutlet` would be wired up as a `UILabel?` optional type. Implicitly unwrapped optional types are used when the variable is known to never be `nil` at runtime, which is usually the case for `@IBOutlet` references. Generally, all `@IBOutlet` references should be implicitly unwrapped optionals.

Summary

This chapter presented two sample iOS applications, one in which the UI was created programmatically and another in which the UI was loaded from a storyboard. Together with an overview of classes, protocols, and enums and an explanation of how iOS applications start, this chapter gives a springboard to understand the Xcode templates that are frequently used to start new projects.

The next chapter, *Storyboard Applications with Swift and iOS*, will go into more detail about how storyboards are created and how an application can be built from scratch.

4

Storyboard Applications with Swift and iOS

Storyboards were introduced in Xcode 4.2 with iOS 5.0. Storyboards solved the problem of being able to graphically present the flow of screens in an iOS application and also provided a way to edit the content of those screens in one place instead of many separate xib files. Storyboards work in the same way with Swift as with Objective-C, and the *Swift and Storyboards* section shows how to integrate Swift code with storyboard transitions.

This chapter will present the following topics:

- How to create a storyboard project
- Creating multiple scenes
- Using segues to navigate between scenes
- Writing custom view controllers
- Connecting views to outlets in Swift
- Laying out views with Auto Layout
- Using constraints to build resizable views

Storyboards, scenes, and segues

By default, Xcode 6 creates a `Main.storyboard` file instead of a `MainWindow.xib` file for newly-created iOS projects. A new `UIMainStoryboardFile` key in the `Info.plist` file points to the application's main storyboard name (without the extension). When the application starts up, `Main.storyboard` is loaded instead of the `NSMainNib` entry. Prior versions of Xcode allowed developers to opt in or out of storyboards, but with Xcode 6, storyboards are the default and developers cannot easily opt out. It is still possible to use `xib` files for individual sections of an application or to use them to load custom classes for prototype table cells. In addition, Xcode 6 creates a `LaunchScreen.xib` to display as a splash screen (on iOS 8 and higher) while the application is loading, in preference to pre-rendered screens at fixed resolutions. This allows devices with many different resolutions (including future unannounced ones) to render pixel-perfect splash screens without having to be rendered at different resolutions for each new device size.

A **storyboard** is a collection of **scenes** (separate screens) that are connected with **segues** (pronounced *segways*). Each scene is represented by a **view controller**, which has an associated **view**. Segues transition between different scenes, with a customizable user interface transition such as a slide or fade, and can be triggered from a UI control or programmatically.

Creating a storyboard project

Since the default templates with Xcode 6 use storyboards by default, any of the existing templates will work. In fact, each of the application templates set up a specific type of view controller and template code. The simplest template to work with and customize is the Single View Application, which can be selected by going to the **File | New | Project...** menu. Create a project called `Storyboards`, which uses a single view application, for experimentation with this chapter. (Refer to the *Creating a single view iOS application* section in *Chapter 3, Creating an iOS Swift App*, for more details on how to create a new application.)

Scenes and view controllers

Standard view controllers can be used to build up an application, which include:

- Split views using a `UISplitViewController` class, which can contain any of the below, but may not be embedded in any other view controller

- Tabbed views using a `UITabBarController` class, which can contain any of the below, but may only be embedded in a split view or used as the root controller

- Navigational controls can be added to existing controllers with a `UINavigationController` class, which can contain any of the below and may be embedded in any of the above or used as a root view controller

- Paginated views using a `UIPageViewController` class, which provide both sliding and page curling display options

- Tabular views using a `UITableViewController` class

- Grid views using a `UICollectionViewController` class

- Audio-visual content using a `AVPlayerViewController` class

- OpenGL ES content using a `GLKViewController` class

- Custom controller content can be represented in a `UIViewController` class or a custom subclass

These classes can be mixed, but there is an explicit ordering that must be followed to satisfy the Apple **Human Interface Guidelines** (also known as the **HIG**). These are all optional, but if combined, they need to obey this ordering:

In addition to the standard view controller classes, custom subclasses can be used as well. This is covered in more detail in the *Custom view controllers* section later in this chapter.

Adding views to the scene

The `Main.storyboard` file can be opened by double-clicking on the file in the project navigator. An editor will open, which shows the storyboard as a set of scenes, along with the document outline on the left. In a single page application, only one view controller will exist.

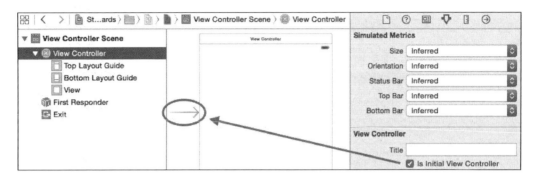

The arrow to the left of the view controller indicates that this scene is the **initial view controller**. This can also be set with the **Is Initial View Controller** checkbox, which can be seen by selecting the **View Controller** from the scene and navigating to the **attributes inspector** (go to **View | Utilities | Show Attributes Inspector**, or press *Command + Option + 4*). The initial view controller can also be changed to a different scene by dragging and dropping the arrow to point to a different scene. Views are added by dragging and dropping them from the **object library** on the bottom-right of Xcode. The object library can be shown by navigating to **View | Utilities | Show Object Library** or by pressing *Command + Option + Control + 3*. Click on a view such as the **Label**, and drag it into the view:

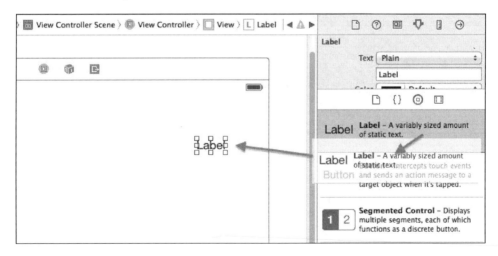

The label's text content can be modified by double-clicking on the label in the view and typing, or by selecting the object and editing the text attribute in the attributes inspector:

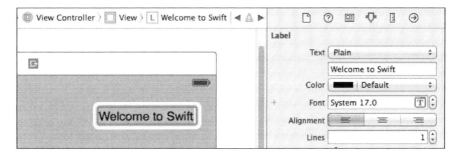

When the element is dragged around, blue guide lines may be seen. These suggest locations for the views; the standard is to have a 20 pt gap between the views and the edge of the screen and an 8 pt gap between adjacent views.

Drag the **Welcome to Swift** label to the top-left of the scene and then drag a **Button** from the object library into the scene. Rename the button's title to **Press Me**. The button should be a standard space (8 pt) away from the label and aligned at the baseline (the level at which the text naturally sits).

At this point, the text in the views is hard-coded in the user interface file and the alignment is manual, which means that the views will not resize if the parent view is modified. These problems will be addressed in the *Connecting views to outlets in Swift* and *Using Auto Layout* sections later in this chapter.

To view the storyboard in the simulator, click on the **Play** button at the top or press *Command + R* to run the application. A window should be shown with **Welcome to Swift** and **Press Me**. At this stage, pressing the button will have no effect, which will be fixed in the next section.

Segues

A **segue** is a transition to a different scene in a storyboard. Segues can be hooked up to views on the screen or can be shown indirectly via code. The most common transitions are when the user has selected a view in the user interface, such as a button, a table row, or a details icon, and a new scene is displayed.

To demonstrate a segue, a new scene is required. Drag a **View Controller** from the object library and drop it onto the storyboard. The exact location of the view controller doesn't matter, but conventionally, scenes are organized from left-to-right in the order in which they will be viewed, so dropping it on the right-hand side of the existing view controller is recommended, as shown here:

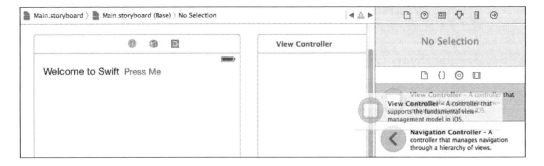

Once the view controller has been added, drop a label onto the top-left and change the text to **Please do not press this button again**. This will present a visual clue that the screen has changed when the segue is followed.

Now, select the **Press Me** button and press the *Control* key while dragging the mouse to the newly created view controller. When the mouse button is released, a pop-up menu will be shown with a number of options, grouped into **Action Segue** and **Non-Adaptive Action Segue**. The former should be used in Xcode 6; the latter is only there for backward compatibility and might be removed in the future.

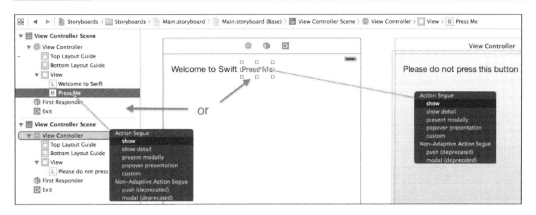

 Alternatively, the object can be selected from the **document outline** on the left, and dragged to the object below in the document outline. It is possible to drag from the view in the editor area to an object in the document outline and vice versa. Dragging to the document outline is sometimes faster and more accurate, especially when there are multiple scenes in a storyboard. The document outline can be shown by navigating to **Editor | Show Document Outline** if it is not visible or by clicking on the icon in the bottom-left of the editor.

Choose the **show** option and a segue will be created between the two views. This is represented as an arrow connecting them and another object in the document outline. The icon inside the circular segue line shows what kind of transition will occur; **push** will have an arrow pointing to the left, while **present modally** will be represented as a square box. The **popover** type will show a small popover icon in the segue.

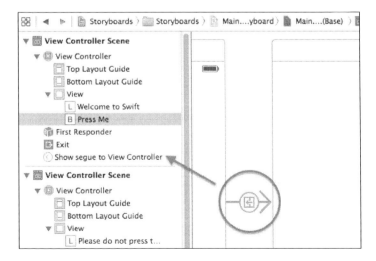

Run the application in the simulator and click on the **Press Me** button. A window should slide up and display the second message.

 There will be no way to dismiss or exit the second screen. This is intentional and will be fixed in the next section.

Adding a navigation controller

When there are multiple screens to be displayed, a parent controller is required to keep track of which screen is currently being shown and what the next step (or previous step) is. This is the purpose of a **navigation controller**; although it has no direct visual representation, it is represented as a scene in a storyboard and can affect the layout of the individual elements in the storyboard.

To embed the initial scene into a navigation controller, select the initial view and navigate to **Editor | Embed In | Navigation Controller**. This will create a new navigation controller view and place it to the left-hand side of the first scene. It will also change the initial view controller to be the navigation controller and set up a **relationship segue** with the name **root view controller** between the navigation controller and the first scene, represented by an icon similar to a percent symbol but with the line rotated the other way, as shown here:

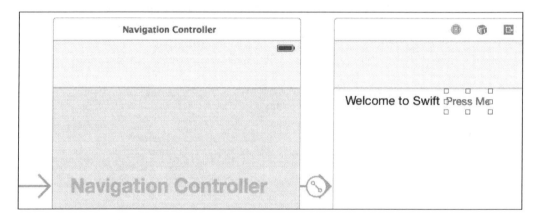

It will be necessary to move the label and button below the newly added navigation bar so that they are still visible. This can either be done before the navigation controller is introduced or by selecting through overlapping objects.

To temporarily hide the navigation bar, delete the relationship segue between the navigation controller and the welcome scene, and the navigation bar will disappear. This will allow the objects to be selected and moved elsewhere temporarily in order to be repositioned. To add it back again, press the *Control* key and drag the mouse cursor from the navigation controller to the welcome scene and choose **root view controller** under **Relationship Segue**.

Alternatively, to select through overlapping objects, first select the object in the document outline so that the location is shown with the drag boxes. Then, press down the *Shift* key and right-click on it for a pop-up menu of the objects under the mouse position at any depth. From here, the object can be selected and then moved with the arrow keys to reposition it elsewhere.

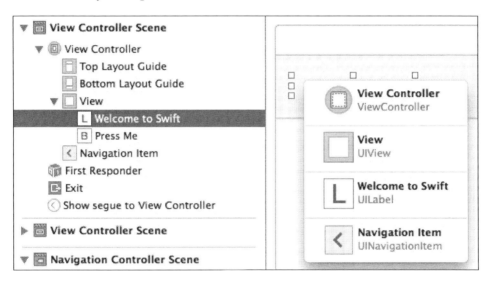

Now, when the application is run and the **Press Me** button is tapped, the message will be shown again but with a **< Back** navigation menu item as well, as shown here:

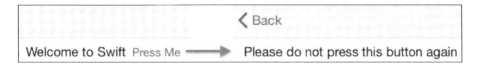

Naming scenes and views

When working with many scenes, calling all of them **View Controller Scene** is not helpful. To distinguish between them, the controllers can be renamed in the storyboard editor.

To change the name of a scene, select its view controller in the document outline and go to **View | Utilities | Show Attributes Inspector**, or press *Command + Option + 3* and then drill down to the **Document** section, where the label hint will read **Xcode Specific Label**. Typing in another value, such as Press Me, Message, or Initial will rename both the view controller and the scene in the document outline:

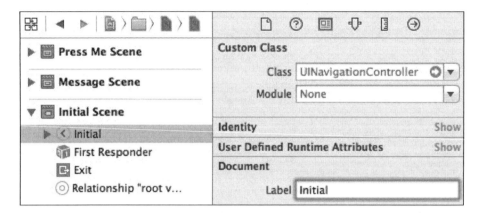

 By default, the name of the element in the document outline is taken from the text value of the element or the type if no text value is present. This means that updates to the label or button text will be automatically reflected in the outline. However, it is possible to add document labels to any view in the document outline.

Swift and storyboards

So far in this chapter, the storyboard content does not involve any Swift or other programming content—it used the drag and drop capabilities of the storyboard editor. Fortunately, it is easy to integrate Storyboard and Swift using a **custom view controller**.

Custom view controllers

Each standard view controller has a corresponding superclass (listed in the *Scenes and view controllers* section previously in this chapter). This can be replaced with a custom subclass, which then has the ability to influence and change what happens in the user interface. To replace the message in the **Message Scene**, create a new file named `MessageViewCotroller.swift` with the following content:

```
import UIKit
class MessageViewController: UIViewController {
}
```

Having created the class, it can be associated with the view controller by selecting it in the storyboard and then switching to the identity inspector by navigating to **View | Utilities | Show Identity Inspector** or pressing *Command + Option + 3*. In the **Custom Class** section, the **Class** will show `UIViewController` as a hint; entering `MessageViewController` here will associate the custom controller with the view controller:

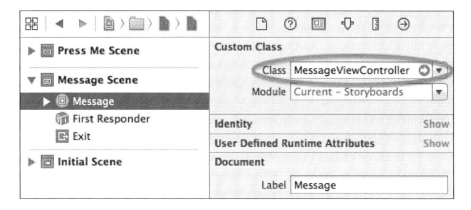

This will have no visible impact to the message scene; running the application will be the same as before. To show a difference, create a `viewDidLoad` method with an `override` keyword and then create a random color for the background:

```
override func viewDidLoad() {
  super.viewDidLoad()
  let red = CGFloat(drand48())
  let green = CGFloat(drand48())
  let blue = CGFloat(drand48())
  view.backgroundColor = UIColor(
    red:red,
    green:green,
```

```
    blue:blue,
    alpha:1.0
  )
}
```

Running the application and pressing the **Press Me** button results in a differently colored view being created each time.

 This does not demonstrate good user experience, but is used here to demonstrate the fact that viewDidLoad is called each time the segue occurs. It is typically used to set up view state just before showing the view to the user.

Connecting views to outlets in Swift

Each view controller has an implicit relationship with its view, and each view has its own backgroundColor property. This example will work regardless of what the view happens to be. What if the view controller needs to interact with the view's content in some way? The view controller could walk the view programmatically, looking for a certain type of view or for a view with a particular identifier, but there is a better way to do this.

Both interface builder and storyboard have the concept of **outlets**, which are a predefined point in a class that can be exposed and can have connections between the UI and the code. In Objective-C, this was done with an IBOutlet qualifier. In Swift, this is done with an @IBOutlet attribute. In effect, they are variables that can be bound to the UI.

 When defining a class with an @IBOutlet attribute, the @objc attribute is also implicitly added, marking this Swift class as using the Objective-C runtime. Since all the UIKit classes are already Objective-C types, this doesn't matter; but for types where the Objective-C runtime should not be used, care should be taken when adding attributes such as @IBOutlet. The @objc attribute can also be used for non-UI classes that need to use the Objective-C runtime.

The following steps are required to create an outlet in a Swift view controller:

1. Define an outlet in the view controller code with @IBOutlet weak var of an optional type of the connected view.

2. Connect the outlet in the view controller to the view by pressing *Control* and dragging the mouse cursor from the view to the outlet.

To do this, open the **assistant editor** by pressing *Command + Option + Enter* or by going to **View | Assistant Editor | Show Assistant Editor**. This will show a side-by-side view of the associated source file. This is useful for showing the associated custom view controller for a selected view in the storyboard (or the interface file).

Once the assistant editor is shown, open the **Message Scene** from the storyboard and press *Control* while dragging the mouse cursor from the message label to the assistant editor and dropping it just after the class declaration:

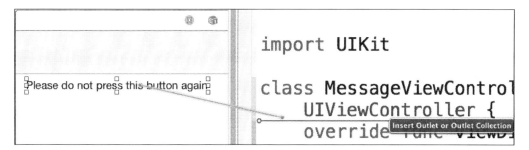

A pop-up dialog will ask what to call the field and present some other information; ensure **Outlet** is selected, name it message, and ensure that it has a **Weak** storage type:

This will result in the following line being added to the `MessageViewController` class, and will wire up the label to the property:

```
class MessageViewController: UIViewController {
  @IBOutlet weak var message: UILabel!

  ...
}
```

The `@IBOutlet` attribute (defined in `UIKit`) allows interface builder to bind to the property. The **weak** storage type—which can be changed in the pop-up dialog—indicates that this class will not hold a strong reference to the object so that when the view is dismissed, the controller will not own it.

Generally, all `@IBOutlet` connections should be marked as `weak`, because the storyboard or `xib` file is the owner of the object, not the controller. Ownership does not pass when assigning properties from interface builder. Changing it to something other than `weak` might lead to circular references. Since Swift uses a reference counting approach to determine when an object is no longer referenced, a circular reference between strong references can cause memory leaks.

The exclamation mark on the end of the type `UILabel!` indicates that it is an **implicitly unwrapped optional**. The property is stored as an optional type, but the accessor code will automatically unwrap it at the point of use. Since the view controller will not have a reference to the `message` at the point of initialization, it will be `nil`, so it must be stored as an optional. However, since accessing the value is known to not be `nil` after the view has been loaded, the implicitly unwrapped optional saves the `?.` calls that will otherwise have to be used each time it is used.

An implicitly unwrapped optional is still an optional value under the covers; it is syntactic sugar for unwrapping it at the point of use each time the value is accessed. When the view is loaded, but before the `viewDidLoad` method is called, the outlet's value will be wired to the instantiated view on screen.

The connections can be seen in the connections inspector, which can be shown by selecting the message label and pressing *Command + Option + 6* or by navigating to **View | Utilities | Show Connections Inspector**. The inspector can also be used to remove existing connections or add new ones.

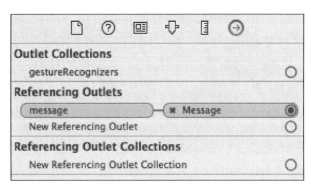

Now that the connection has been made between the message view and the custom controller, instead of changing the background color of the view, change the background color of the `message` instead:

```
message.backgroundColor = UIColor(...)
```

Run the application and the message will have the background color changed each time the scene is shown:

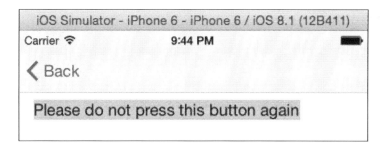

Calling actions from interface builder

In the same way that outlets are variables for interface builder to assign to (or read from), **actions** are methods/functions that can be triggered from a view in interface builder. The `@IBAction` attribute is used to annotate a method or function that can be wired up.

 As with `@IBOutlet`, using `@IBAction` on a function causes the compiler to implicitly add an `@objc` attribute to the class, in order to force it to use the Objective-C runtime.

To change the message when a button is invoked, a suitable `changeMessage` is required. Historically, the signature for an action method was one that returned `void`, marked with `IBAction`, and took a `sender` argument, which could be any object. In Swift, this signature translates to:

```
@IBAction func changeMessage(sender:AnyObject) { … }
```

However, with Swift, the `sender` is no longer a required argument. It is therefore possible to bind an action with the following signature:

```
@IBAction func changeMessage() { … }
```

If the signature is changed, any existing bindings must be deleted and recreated as an error will be reported otherwise.

It is difficult to convert from a `func` that doesn't take an argument to one that takes an argument. It is easier to have a `func` that takes an argument that isn't required. If not sure, choose the function signature that takes a sender object and then just ignore it.

The `changeMessage` function can randomly select a message and set the text on the label:

```
let messages = [
    "Ouch, that hurts",
    "Please don't do that again",
    "Why did you press that?",
]
@IBAction func changeMessage() {
    message.text = messages[
        Int(arc4random_uniform(
            UInt32(messages.count)))]
}
```

When the function is invoked, the message text will change to a value defined in the array. To call the function, it needs to be wired up in the storyboard editor. Add a new **Button** from the object library to the message scene, with a `Change Message` label. To connect it to the action, press *Control* and drag the mouse cursor from the **Change Message** button in the **Message Scene** and drop it in the **Message** view controller at the top:

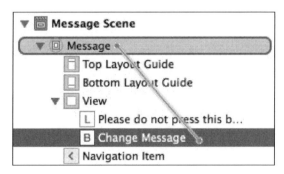

A pop-up menu will then be shown of the outlets and actions that this can be connected to. Select the **changeMessage** from the list:

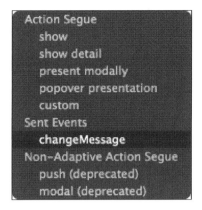

 If `changeMessage` isn't listed, check that the view controller is defined to be the `MessageViewController` and verify that the `@IBAction` attribute is added to the `changeMessage` function.

Now, when the application is run and the **Change Message** button is pressed, the label will change to one of the hard-coded values.

 The message label will not change in size, since the view has no automatic layout associated with it. The *Using Auto Layout* section in this chapter explains how to fix this problem.

Triggering a segue with code

A segue can be triggered programmatically from code, if additional setup is required or there are data parameters that need to be passed from one view controller to another (such as the currently selected object).

Segues have named **segue identifiers**, which are used in code to trigger specific segues. To test this out, drag a new **View Controller** from the library (by pressing *Command + Option + Control + 3* or by navigating to **View | Utilities | Show Object Library**) onto the main storyboard and name it `About`. Drag a **Label** and give it the text `About this App`.

Next, create a segue by pressing *Control* and dragging the mouse cursor between the **Message** scene to the new scene. The named identifier can be set as about through the attributes inspector (shown by pressing *Command* + *Option* + *4* or by navigating to **View | Utilities | Show Attributes Inspector**):

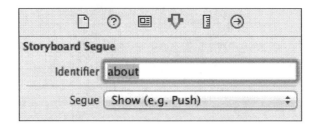

Finally, drag a new **Button** to the **Change Message** scene and call it About. Instead of directly calling the segue, create a new @IBAction called about. When this button is pressed, the following code will be run:

```
@IBAction func about(sender: AnyObject) {
    performSegueWithIdentifier("about", sender: sender)
}
```

When the **About** button is pressed, the about screen will be displayed.

Passing data with segues

Typically in a master-detail application, data needs to be passed from one scene to the next. This might be the currently selected object, or it might require additional information to be processed. When the segue is called, the view controller's prepareForSegue method is called, with the destination segue and the sending object. This allows any internal state of the view controller to be passed to the new segue.

The UIStoryboardSegue contains an identifier, which was set in the previous section. Since the prepareForSegue method might be called on the MessageViewController for any number of segues, it is common for a switch statement to be used on the identifier so that the right action can be taken. For a single segue, an if statement can be used:

```
override func prepareForSegue(segue: UIStoryboardSegue,
    sender: AnyObject?) {
    if segue.identifier == "about" {
        let dest = segue.destinationViewController as UIViewController
        dest.view.backgroundColor = message.backgroundColor
    }
}
```

Here, the `prepareForSegue` method is called with `segue`, which contains the destination (the scene) and the identifier. The `if` statement ensures that the correct identifier is matched. In this case, the background color of the message label (which is chosen randomly when the view is loaded) is passed to the destination view's background color; however, any property on either the view controller or the view can be set here.

Using Auto Layout

Auto Layout has been part of Xcode for the last few releases, and it was added to support an evolution from the previous springs and struts approach that predated Mac OS X. First released on iOS in 6.0, it has evolved to the point where size-independent displays can now be created as the default.

Understanding constraints

In Xcode 5, interface builder enabled Auto Layout by default for the first time. When a label was dragged to the top or bottom of the parent view, a dotted blue line would indicate that the label was correctly spaced, and a **constraint** would be generated.

However, in many cases, the constraints weren't created correctly or had undesired effects. For example, positioning a button in the center at the top might not maintain the location depending on whether the constraint being added was absolute (200 px from the right) or relative (in the center of the screen). In both cases, the button might look like it was positioned correctly, only to fail when the device's screen orientation rotates or it is run on a screen of different size.

In Xcode 6, although the guidelines are still shown as views are moved around, relative constraints are not created. Instead, each view is given an exact hardcoded position that does not change with screen rotation or with a change of display size.

Constraints must be added manually to the views in order to restore the right behavior, and as manual constraints are added, absolute constraints are removed.

Adding constraints

In the example application, the **Welcome to Swift** label and the **Press Me** button are next to each other, a small distance from the top. However, when the screen is rotated in the simulator, by pressing *Command* and the left or right arrow keys, the spacing between the labels and the top doesn't change, so the labels look further away.

The desired outcome is that the label remain a standard distance away from the top-left and the button remain aligned to the label's baseline.

There are two separate constraints that need to be applied to the label:

- Be a standard vertical distance away from the top of the parent view
- Be a standard horizontal distance away from the left of the parent view

There are also two constraints that need to be applied to the button:

- Be aligned with the label's baseline
- Be a standard vertical distance away from the label

There are different ways of adding a constraint, which are covered in the following sections.

Adding a constraint with the drag and drop method

A quick way to add a constraint is to press *Control* and drag the mouse cursor from the view to the top of the container. Depending on the direction of the drag, different options will be shown. Dragging vertically upwards presents the vertical alignment options:

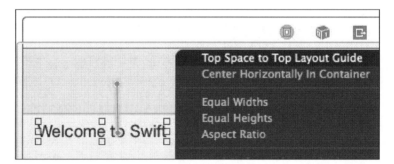

The **Top Space to Top Layout Guide** option will insert a recommended break between the navigation bar and the label. There is a **Center Horizontally in Container** option, which is also a vertical separation but not appropriate in this case.

The other types that are active — **Equal Widths, Equal Heights**, and **Aspect Ratio** — allow multiple views to be sized relative to each other.

Dragging horizontally will show a different set of options at the top, including **Leading Space to Container Margin** and **Center Vertically in Container**:

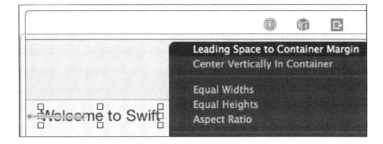

If the mouse is dragged at an angle, both sets of options will be shown:

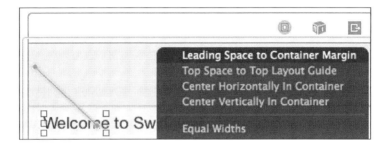

Adding constraints to the Press Me scene

To set the constraints for the welcome label, press *Control* and drag the mouse cursor from the label to the left and select **Leading Space to Container Margin**. An orange line will appear, and a dotted outline will be shown at the top of the screen.

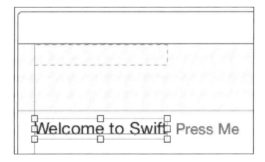

The orange line indicates an **ambiguous constraint**, which indicates some constraints have been added to the view but are not enough to uniquely position the label. In this case, the label is positioned from the left of the container, but it could be anywhere with respect to the top or bottom of the screen. The red dotted lines show where the Auto Layout algorithm will put the view with the constraints currently specified.

To resolve this problem, press *Control* and drag the mouse pointer from the label to the top and select **Top Space to Top Layout Guide**. Once this is done, two constraints will be shown in blue, which represent the constraints about the object:

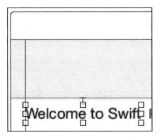

The constraints can also be seen in the document outline on the left-hand side:

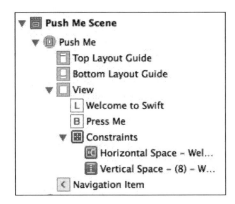

If the application is run now and rotated, the label is correctly repositioned but the button is not:

Adding missing constraints

To find which views have no constraints, click through the views one by one in the document outline and check the size inspector (which can be seen by pressing *Command + Option + 5* or by navigating to **View** | **Utilities** | **Show Size Inspector**). For views that have constraints set, there will be content shown under the **Constraints** section:

If a view has no constraints associated with it, then this section will be empty.

Interface builder has an option to create missing constraints for selected views, which can be accessed by navigating to **Editor** | **Resolve Auto Layout Issues** | **Add Missing Constraints** or from the **Resolve Auto Layout Issues** menu at the bottom-right, which looks like a triangle between two vertical lines.

When selected, the options in the top-half apply to selected views only, while the options in the bottom-half work on all the views in the selected view controller.

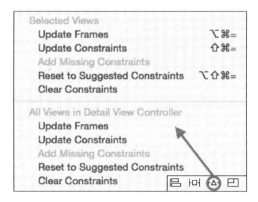

The options include:

- **Update Frames**: This is based on the current constraints; it automatically repositions and resizes the views to correspond to what will happen at runtime

- **Update Constraints**: This is based on the current positions of the objects and attempts to recalculate the existing constraints (but not create new ones)

- **Add Missing Constraints**: This is based on the approximate positioning of the components and adds constraints that create the same result

- **Reset to Suggested Constraints**: This is equivalent to clearing all the constraints associated with the views and then readding missing constraints

- **Clear Constraints**: This removes all the constraints associated with the views

To add constraints to the **Press Me** button, click on the view and then navigate to **Editor | Resolve Auto Layout Issues | Selected Views | Add Missing Constraints**. There should be two constraints added: a baseline alignment with the label and a horizontal space to the label.

To see the effect of the **Update Frames** operation, move the label and the button to different places in the view controller. Orange lines and dotted outlines will be shown, indicating that there is an ambiguous constraint. Navigate to **Choose Editor | Resolve Auto Layout Issues | All Views in View Controller | Update Frames**, and the views will automatically move to the right places and resize.

The views are sized to their **intrinsic size**, which is the size that just fits the content. For example, a label's intrinsic size is the size in which the text can fit into the space in the current font. This can be used to fix the size of the label in the **Message Scene**; by adding constraints, the changing text will result in the intrinsic size being recalculated, and the background color will be correctly sized.

Now, run the application and rotate the device by pressing *Command* and the left and right arrow keys to see the view resize itself correctly.

Summary

This chapter introduced the concept of storyboards as a sequence of scenes that are connected with segues, which can either be wired with the GUI or driven programmatically. Finally, Auto Layout can be used to build applications that respond to differences in screen orientation or size as well as respond to changes in view size or other properties.

The next chapter will present how to create custom views in Swift.

5

Creating Custom Views in Swift

User interfaces can be built by combining standard views and view controllers through interface builder, storyboard editor, or custom code. However, it will eventually become necessary to break apart a user interface into smaller, reusable, and easier-to-test segments. These are known as **custom views**.

This chapter will present the following topics:

- Customizing table views
- Building and laying out custom view subclasses
- Drawing graphical views with drawRect
- Creating layered graphics with animation

An overview of UIView

All iOS views are rooted in an Objective-C class called `UIView`, which comes from the UIKit framework/module. The `UIView` class represents a rectangular space that might be associated with `UIWindow` or constructed to represent an off-screen view. Views that perform user interactions are generally subclasses of `UIControl`. Both `UIView` and `UIViewController` inherit from the `UIResponder` class, which in turn inherits from `NSObject`.

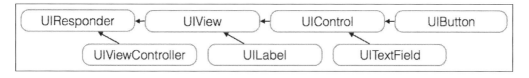

On Mac OS X, views are rooted in NSView and come from the AppKit framework. Otherwise, the two implementations are very similar.

A new Xcode project will be used to create custom view classes. Create a new project with a **Tabbed View Application** template called CustomViews. To start with a blank sheet, delete the generated view controllers and the associated FirstViewController and SecondViewController classes.

Creating new views with interface builder

The easiest way of creating a custom view is to use interface builder to drag and drop the contents. This is typically done with a UITableView and a **prototype table cell**.

Creating a table view controller

Drag in the table view controller from the object library onto the main storyboard, and drag and drop from the tab bar controller to the newly created table view controller to create a relation segue called view controllers. (Segues are covered in more detail in the *Storyboards, Segues, and Scenes* section in *Chapter 4, Storyboard Applications with Swift and iOS*)

By default, the table view controller will have **dynamic property content** — that is, it will be able to display a variable number of rows. This is defined in the **Table View** section of the **Attributes Inspector**.

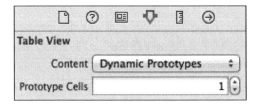

 There is an option for tables to have **static content**; a fixed number of rows in the table. This is sometimes useful when creating scrollable content that can be partitioned into slices, even if it doesn't look like a table. Most of the elements in the iOS settings are represented as a fixed-size table view.

At the top of the table view are one or more **prototype cells**. These are used to define the look and feel of the table items. By default, a `UITableViewCell` is used, which has a label and an image, but a prototype cell can be used to add more data to the entries.

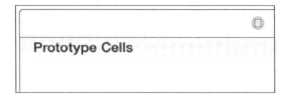

The prototype cell can be used to provide additional information or views. For example, two labels can be dragged into the view; one label can be centered at the top and can be displayed in the headline font, while the second can be left aligned.

Drag two labels from the object library into the prototype cell. Arrange them using Auto Layout appropriately.

To change a label's font, select the label in the editor and go to the **Attributes Inspector**. In the **Label** section, click on the font chooser icon and select **Headline** or **Subhead**, as appropriate.

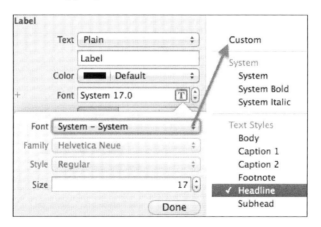

When finished, the prototype cell will look like:

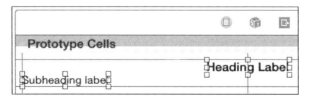

When the application is run, an empty table will be seen. This is because the table doesn't have any items displayed at the moment. The next section shows how to add data to a table so that it binds and displays items to the prototype cell.

Showing data in the table

A UITableView acquires data from a UITableViewDataSource. The UITableViewController class already implements the UITableViewDataSource protocol, so only a small number of methods are required to provide data for the table.

 Because UITableView was originally implemented in Objective-C, the methods defined in the protocol take a tableView. As a result, all of the UITableViewDataSource delegate methods in Swift end up being called tableView with different arguments.

Create a new SampleTable class that extends UITableViewController. Implement the class as follows:

```
import UIKit
class SampleTable: UITableViewController {
  var items = [
    ("First", "A first item"),
    ("Second", "A second item"),
  ]
  required init(coder:NSCoder) {
    super.init(coder:coder)
  }
  override func tableView(tableView: UITableView,
    numberOfRowsInSection section:Int) -> Int {
    return items.count
  }
  override func tableView(tableView: UITableView,
    cellForRowAtIndexPath indexPath: NSIndexPath)
      -> UITableViewCell {
    let cell = tableView.
    dequeueReusableCellWithIdentifier("prototypeCell")
    as UITableViewCell
    // configure labels
    return cell
  }
}
```

Once the data source methods are implemented, the labels need to be configured to display the data from the array. There are three things that need to be done: the prototype cell must be acquired from the `xib` file; the labels need to be extracted; and finally the table view controller needs to be associated with the custom `SampleTable` class.

Firstly, the `cellForRowAtIndex` function needs an identifier for reusable cells. The **identifier** is set on the prototype cell in the main storyboard. To set it, select the prototype cell and go to the **Attributes Inspector**. Enter `prototypeCell` in the **Identifier** of the **Table View Cell** section:

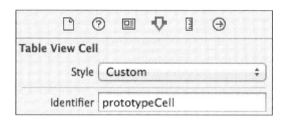

The identifier is used in the `dequeueReusableCellWithIdentifier` method of the `tableView`. When a `xib` is used to load the cell, the return value will either reuse a cell that has gone off-screen earlier or a new cell will be instantiated from `xib`.

Each label can be given a non-zero integer **tag** so that the label can be extracted from the prototype cell using the `viewWithTag` method:

```
let titleLabel = cell.viewWithTag(1) as UILabel
let subtitleLabel = cell.viewWithTag(2) as UILabel
```

To assign tags to the views, select the `heading` label, navigate to the **Attributes Inspector**, and change the **Tag** to 1. Do the same thing for the `subheading` label with the tag 2.

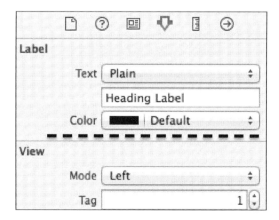

Now the text values for the row can be set:

```
let (title,subtitle) = items[indexPath.row]
titleLabel.text = title
subtitleLabel.text = subtitle
```

Finally, the `SampleTable` needs to be associated with the table view controller. Click on the table, go to the **Identity Inspector**, and enter `SampleTable` in the **Custom Class** section.

When the application is run, the following view will be shown:

 To hide the status bar, add or change **Status bar is initially hidden** to **YES** and **View controller-based status bar appearance** to **NO** in the `Info.plist` file.

Defining a view in a XIB file

It is possible to create a view using interface builder, save it as a `xib` file, and then instantiate it on demand. This is what happens under the covers with the `UITableView`—there is a method `registerNib:forCellReuseIdentifier:` which takes an `xib` file and an identifier (which corresponds to `prototypeCell` in the previous example).

Create a new interface file `CounterView.xib` to represent the view, by navigating to **File | New | File | iOS | User Interface | View**. When opened, it will show as an empty view with no content and in a 600 x 600 square. To change the size to something that is a little more reasonable, go to the **Attributes Inspector** and change the size from **Inferred** to **Freeform**. At the same time, change the **Status Bar**, **Top Bar**, and **Bottom Bar** to **None**. Then, change to the **Size Inspector** and modify the view's **Frame Rectangle** to 300 x 50.

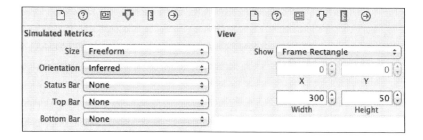

This should resize the view so that it is displayed as 300 x 50 instead of the previous 600 x 600, and the status bar and other bars should not be seen. Now, add a **Stepper** from the object library by dragging it to the left-hand side of the view and dragging a **Label** to the right. Adjust the size and add the missing constraints so that the view looks similar to the following screenshot:

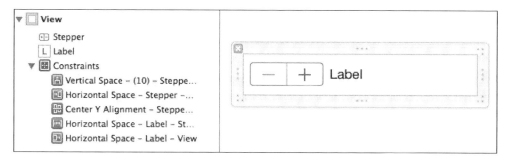

Wiring a custom view class

Create a new `CounterView` class that extends `UIView`, define an `@IBOutlet` for the `label` and an `@IBAction change` method that takes a `sender`. Wire the stepper's `valueChanged` event to the `change` method and connect the `label` outlet. Implement the `change` function such that the label text is changed when the stepper is picked:

```
import UIKit
class CounterView: UIView {
  @IBOutlet weak var label:UILabel!
  @IBAction func change(sender:AnyObject) {
    let count = (sender as UIStepper).value
    label.text = "Count is \(count)"
  }
}
```

The CounterView will be added to the **table header** of the SampleTable. Each UITableViewController has a reference to its associated UITableView, and each UITableView has an optional headerView (and footerView) that is used for the table as a whole.

The UITableView also has a sectionHeader and a sectionFooter, which are used to separate different sections of the table. A table can have multiple sections — for example, one section per month — and a separate header and footer can be used per section.

To create a CounterView, the xib file must be loaded. This is done by instantiating a UINib with a nibName and a bundle. The most appropriate place to do this is in the viewDidLoad method of the SampleTable class:

```
class SampleTable: UITableViewController {
  override func viewDidLoad() {
    let xib = UINib(nibName:"CounterView", bundle:nil)
    // continued
```

Once the xib is loaded, the view must be created. The instantiateWithOwner method allows the object(s) in the xib to be deserialized.

It is possible to store multiple objects in a xib file (for example, to define a separate view that is suitable for a small display device versus a big display device) but in general a xib file only contains one view.

The owner is passed to the view so that any connections can be wired up to the **File's Owner** in the interface. This is typically either self or nil if there are no connections.

```
// continued from before
let objects = xib.instantiateWithOwner(self, options:nil)
// continued
```

This returns an array of AnyObject instances, so casting the first element to a UIView is a common step.

It is possible to use objects[0], but this will cause a failure if the array is empty. Instead, use objects.first to get an optional value containing the first element.

Using the `as?` cast, it is possible to convert the optional value to a more specific type, and from that perform the assignment to the `tableHeaderView`:

```
// continued from before
let counter = objects.first as? UIView
tableView.tableHeaderView = counter
}
```

When the application is run in the simulator, the header is seen at the top of the table:

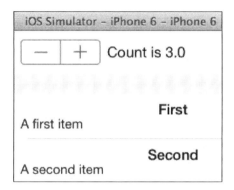

One of the advantages of having a `xib` for representing the user interface is that it can be reused in many places with a single definition. For example, it is possible to use the same `xib` to instantiate another view for the footer of the table:

```
tableView.tableFooterView =
    xib.instantiateWithOwner(self,options:nil).first as? UIView
```

When the application is run now, counters are created at the top and bottom of the table:

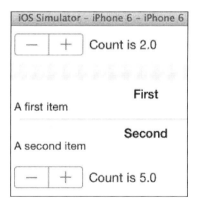

Dealing with intrinsic size

When a view is added into a view that is being managed with Auto Layout, its **intrinsic content size** is used. Unfortunately, views defined in interface builder have no way of setting their intrinsic size programmatically or of specifying it in interface builder. The **Size Inspector** allows this value to be changed, but as Xcode notes, this has no effect at runtime:

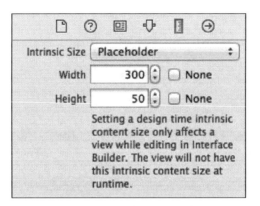

If a custom class is associated with the view, then an appropriate intrinsic size can be defined. Add a method to `CounterView` that overrides the `intrinsicContentSize` method and returns a `CGSize`, and to allow for some `xib` customization, return the maximum of the label's intrinsic size and a value such as `(300,50)`:

```
override func intrinsicContentSize() -> CGSize {
    let height = max(50,label.intrinsicContentSize().height)
    let width = max(300,label.intrinsicContentSize().width)
    return CGSize(width: width, height: height)
}
```

Now when the `CounterView` is added into a view that is managed by Auto Layout, it will have an appropriate initial size, although it can grow larger.

The size should take into account the size of the various views contained inside as well as any font sizes or themes, which might change the view. Using the label's `intrinsicSize` to calculate a maximum is a good idea.

Creating views by subclassing UIView

Although `xib` files offer a mechanism to customize classes, the majority of UIKit views outside of standard frameworks are implemented in custom code. This makes it easier to reason what the intrinsic size should be as well as to receive code patches and understand diffs from version control systems. The downside of this approach is when using Auto Layout, writing the constraints can be a challenge and the intrinsic sizes are often misreported or return the unknown value (`-1,-1`).

A custom view can be implemented as a subclass of `UIView`. Subclasses of `UIView` are expected to have two initializers; one that takes `frame:CGRect` and one that takes a `coder:NSCoder`. The `frame` is generally used in code, and the `rect` specifies the position on screen (`0,0` is the top-left) along with the `width` and `height`. The `coder` is used when deserializing from a `xib` file.

To allow custom subclasses to be used in either interface builder or instantiated from code, it is a best practice to ensure that both the initializers create the necessary views. This can be done by using a third method, called something similar to `setupUI`, that is invoked from both.

Create a class called `TwoLabels` that has two labels in a view:

```
import UIKit
class TwoLabels: UIView {
  var left:UILabel = UILabel()
  var right:UILabel = UILabel()
  required init(coder:NSCoder) {
    super.init(coder:coder)
    setupUI()
  }
  override init(frame:CGRect) {
    super.init(frame:frame)
    setupUI()
  }
  // ...
}
```

The `setupUI` call will add the subviews to the view. Code that goes in here should be executed only once. There isn't a standard name, and often example code will put the setup in one or other of the `init` methods instead.

It is conventional to have a separate method such as updateUI to populate the UI with the current set of data. This can be called repeatedly based on the state of the system; for example, a field might be enabled or disabled based on some condition. This code should be repeatable so that it does not modify the view hierarchy:

```
func setupUI() {
  addSubview(left)
  addSubview(right)
  updateUI()
}
func updateUI() {
  left.text = "Left"
  right.text = "Right"
}
```

In an explicitly sized environment (where the text label is being set and placed at a particular location), there is a layoutSubviews method that is called to request the view to be laid out correctly. However, there is a better way to do this, which is to use Auto Layout and constraints.

Auto Layout and custom views

Auto Layout is covered in the *Using Auto Layout* section of *Chapter 4, Storyboard Applications with Swift and iOS*. When creating a user interface explicitly, views must be sized and managed appropriately. The most appropriate way to manage this is to use Auto Layout, which requires constraints to be added in order to set up the views.

Constraints can be added or updated in the updateConstraints method. This is called after setNeedsUpdateConstraints is called. Constraints might need to be updated if views become visible or the data is changed. Typically, this can be triggered by placing a call at the end of the setupUI method:

```
func setupUI() {
  // addSubview etc
  setNeedsUpdateConstraints()
}
```

The updateConstraints method needs to do several things. To prevent auto-resizing masks being translated into constraints, each view needs to call setTranslatesAutoresizingMaskIntoConstraints with an argument of false.

To facilitate the transition between springs and struts (also known as auto-resizing masks) and Auto Layouts, views can be configured to translate springs and struts into Auto Layout constraints. This is enabled by default for all views in order to provide backward compatibility for existing views, but should be disabled when implementing Auto Layouts.

Either the constraints can be incrementally updated or the existing constraints can be removed. A `removeConstraints` method allows existing constraints to be removed first:

```
override func updateConstraints() {
  setTranslatesAutoresizingMaskIntoConstraints(false)
  left.setTranslatesAutoresizingMaskIntoConstraints(false)
  right.setTranslatesAutoresizingMaskIntoConstraints(false)
  removeConstraints(constraints())
  // add constraints here
}
```

Constraints can be added programmatically using the `NSLayoutConstraint` class. The constraints added in interface builder are also instances of the `NSLayoutConstraint` class.

Constraints are represented as an equation; properties of two objects are related as an equality (or inequality) of the form:

```
// object.property = otherObject.property * multiplier + constant
```

To declare that both labels are of equal width, the following can be added to the `updateConstraints` method:

```
// left.width = right.width * 1 + 0
let equalWidths = NSLayoutConstraint(
  item: left,
  attribute: .Width,
  relatedBy: .Equal,
  toItem: right,
  attribute: .Width,
  multiplier: 1,
  constant: 0)
addConstraint(equalWidths)
```

Constraints and the visual format language

Although adding individual constraints gives ultimate flexibility, it can be tedious to set up programmatically. The **visual format language** can be used to add multiple constraints to a view. This is an ASCII-based representation that allows views to be related to each other in position and extrapolated into an array of constraints.

Constraints can be applied horizontally (the default) or vertically. The | character can be used to represent either the start or end of the containing superview, and – is used to represent the space that separates views, which are named in [] and referenced in a dictionary.

To constrain the two labels that are next to each other in the view, H:|-[left]-[right]-| can be used. This can be read as a horizontal constraint (H:) with a gap from the left edge (|-) followed by the left view ([left]), a gap (-), a right view ([right]), and finally a gap from the right edge (-|). Similarly, vertical constraints can be added with a V: prefix.

The constraintsWithVisualFormat method on the NSLayoutConstraint class can be used to parse visual format constraints. It takes a set of options, metrics, and a dictionary of views referenced in the visual format. An array of constraints is returned, which can be passed into the addConstraints method of the view.

To add constraints that ensure the left and right views have equal widths, a space between them, and a vertical space between the top of the view and the labels, the following code can be used:

```swift
override func updateConstraints() {
  // ...
  let namedViews = ["left":left,"right":right]
  addConstraints(NSLayoutConstraint.
    constraintsWithVisualFormat("H:|-[left]-[right]-|",
      options: nil, metrics: nil, views: namedViews))
  addConstraints(NSLayoutConstraint.
    constraintsWithVisualFormat("V:|-[left]-|",
      options: nil, metrics: nil, views: namedViews))
  addConstraints(NSLayoutConstraint.
    constraintsWithVisualFormat("V:|-[right]-|",
      options: nil, metrics: nil, views: namedViews))
  super.updateConstraints()
}
```

If there are ambiguous constraints, then an error will be printed to the console when the view is shown. Messages that include the **NSAutoresizingMaskLayout constraints** indicate that the view has not disabled the automatic translation of auto-resizing mask into constraints.

Adding the custom view to the table

The `TwoLabels` view can be tested by adding it as a footer to the `SimpleTable` created previously. The footer is a special class, `UITableViewHeaderFooterView`, which needs to be created and added to the `tableView`. The `TwoLabels` view can then be added to the footer's `contentView`:

```
let footer = UITableViewHeaderFooterView()
footer.contentView.addSubview(TwoLabels(frame:CGRect.zeroRect))
tableView.tableFooterView = footer
```

Now, when the application is run in the simulator, the custom view will be seen:

Custom graphics with drawRect

Subclasses of `UIView` can implement their own custom graphics by providing a **drawRect** method that implements the custom drawing routines. The `drawRect` method takes a `CGRect` argument, which indicates the area to draw in, but the actual drawing commands are performed on a Core Graphics **context**, which is represented by the `CGContext` class and can be obtained by a call to `UIGraphicsGetCurrentContext`.

The Core Graphics context represents a drawable area in iOS and is used for printing as well as drawing graphics. Each view is responsible for drawing itself; the rectangle will either be the full area (for example, the first time that a view is drawn) or it might be a subset of the area (for example, when a dialog has been shown and then subsequently removed).

Core Graphics is a C-based interface (rather than Objective-C based), so the API is exposed as a set of functions beginning with the **UIGraphics** prefix. As with other drawing APIs, the program can set the current drawing color, draw lines, set a fill color, fill rectangles, and so on.

To test this, create a class called SquaresView that is a subclass of UIView in a new Swift file.

All views have the standard init methods; delegate them to the superclass' implementation. Finally, create a drawRect method that takes a CGRect. This will be where the custom drawing occurs. The skeleton will look like:

```
import UIKit
class SquaresView: UIView {
  required init(coder: NSCoder) {
    super.init(coder:coder)
    setupUI()
  }
  override init(frame: CGRect) {
    super.init(frame:frame)
    setupUI()
  }
  func setupUI() {
  }
  override func drawRect(rect: CGRect) {
    // drawing code goes here
  }
}
```

Open the Main.storyboard and drag in another UIViewController, and set the custom class of the view to SquaresView in the **Identity Inspector**. Drag in a relationship segue between the tabbed view controller and the new view controller, and set the tab bar item to Squares, which will allow testing to move to a different view. If the application is run, a blank view will be seen in the **Squares** tab.

Drawing graphics in drawRect

To draw graphics in the view, it is necessary to acquire a `CGContext` and then set a drawing (stroke) color. A `UIColor` can be acquired and then converted into a `CGColor` to be able to set it on the graphics context.

A rectangle can be drawn with `CGContextStrokeRect`:

```
override func drawRect(rect: CGRect) {
  let context = UIGraphicsGetCurrentContext()
  let red = UIColor.redColor().CGColor
  CGContextSetStrokeColorWithColor(context, red)
  CGContextStrokeRect(context,
    CGRect(x:50, y:50, width:100, height:100))
}
```

When this is run in the simulator, a red rectangle will be shown on the **Squares** tab.

To draw a green square with a black outline in the middle requires a filled green square to be drawn first, followed by a black square afterwards. (Drawing them in the opposite order will result in the solid green square obliterating the black square.)

There are two different colors in a Core Graphics context: the **stroke color**, which is used to draw lines and paths; and the **fill color**, which is used when creating a filled path. Although the `CGContextSetFillColorWithColor` function exists, in Swift there is an easier way of setting this directly with `UIColor`, using the `setFill` or `setStroke` methods. The following will create the green square with a black border:

```
UIColor.greenColor().setFill()
UIColor.blackColor().setStroke()
CGContextFillRect(context,
  CGRect(x:75, y:75, width:50, height:50))
CGContextStrokeRect(context,
  CGRect(x:75, y:75, width:50, height:50))
```

Now when the application is run, the following screenshot will be seen:

Responding to orientation changes

When the screen rotates, the view is stretched and squashed, resulting in the square turning into a rectangle. The drawRect call is not called when the view changes orientation; the existing display is squashed and stretched automatically.

To prevent this, the **content mode** of the view can be changed. There is a UIViewContentMode enumeration which can be specified to cause different behaviors. Using Redraw will result in the drawRect being called when the orientation changes or when the bounds changes size.

The squares can be centered on the screen; instead of starting at the position 50, 50, the view's center property can be accessed to find what the position is. Modify the code as follows:

```
func setupUI() {
  contentMode = .Redraw
}
override func drawRect(rect: CGRect) {
  let context = UIGraphicsGetCurrentContext()
  let red = UIColor.redColor().CGColor
  CGContextSetStrokeColorWithColor(context,red)
  CGContextStrokeRect(context,
    CGRect(x:center.x-50, y:center.y-50, width:100, height:100))
  UIColor.greenColor().setFill()
  UIColor.blackColor().setStroke()
  CGContextFillRect(context,
    CGRect(x:center.x-25, y:center.y-25, width:50, height:50))
  CGContextStrokeRect(context,
    CGRect(x:center.x-25, y:center.y-25, width:50, height:50))
}
```

Now when the application is run, the squares will be centered in the screen. If the screen rotates, the drawRect will be invoked again and the display will be redrawn.

Custom graphics with layers

Drawing graphics by overriding drawRect is not very performant, because all the drawing routines are executed on the CPU. Offloading the graphics drawing to the GPU is both more performant and more power efficient.

iOS has a concept of layers, which are Core Graphics optimized drawing contents. Operations composed on a **layer**, including adding a **path**, can be translated into code that can execute on the GPU and be rendered efficiently. In addition, Core Animation can be used to animate changes on layers efficiently.

 Core Animation is provided in the **QuartzCore** framework/ module; the two terms are interchangeable. It is more generally known as Core Animation.

The download progress icon on iOS can be recreated as a `ProgressView` containing layers for the circular outline, a layer for the square stop button in the middle, and a layer for the progress arc. The final view will composite these three layers together to provide the finished view.

Every `UIView` has an implicit associated layer, which can have sublayers added to it. As with views, newly added layers overlay existing layers. There are several **core animation layer** classes that can be used, which are subclasses of `CALayer`:

- The `CAEAGLLayer` class provides a way to embed OpenGL content into a view

- The `CAEmitterLayer` class provides a mechanism to generate emitter effects, such as smoke and fire

- The `CAGradientLayer` class provides a way to create a background with a gradient color

- The `CAReplicatorLayer` class provides a means to replicate the existing layers with different transformations, which allows effects such as reflections and coverflow to be shown

- The `CAScrollLayer` class provides a way to perform scrolling

- The `CAShapeLayer` class provides a means to draw and animate a single path

- The `CATextLayer` class allows text to be displayed

- The `CATiledLayer` class provides a means to generate tiled content at different zoom levels, such as a map

- The `CATransformLayer` class provides a means to transform layers into 3D views, such as a coverflow style image animation

Creating a ProgressView from layers

Create another view class called `ProgressView`, which extends `UIView`. Set it up
with the default `init` methods, a `setupUI` and an `updateUI` method:

```
import UIKit
class ProgressView: UIView {
  required init(coder: NSCoder) {
    super.init(coder:coder)
    setupUI()
  }
  override init(frame: CGRect) {
    super.init(frame:frame)
    setupUI()
  }
  func setupUI() {
    updateUI()
  }
  func updateUI() {
  }
}
```

Create a new `Layers Scene` in the `Main.storyboard` by dragging a **View Controller**
from the object library onto the storyboard. Connect it to the tab bar controller by
dragging a relationship segue to the newly created layers view controller. Add the
`ProgressView` by dragging a **View** from the object library and giving it a **Custom
Class** of `ProgressView`. Size it with an approximate location of the middle of
the screen.

Now add an instance variable to the `ProgressView` class called `circle` and create
a new instance of `CAShapeLayer`. In `setupUI` set the `strokeColor` as `black`
and the `fillColor` as `nil`. Finally, add the `circle` layer to the view's layer so that it
is shown:

```
let circle = CAShapeLayer()
func setupUI() {
  circle.strokeColor = UIColor.blackColor().CGColor
  circle.fillColor = nil
  self.layer.addSublayer(circle)
  updateUI()
}
```

A CAShapeLayer has a path property, which is used to perform all the drawing. The easiest way to use this is to create a UIBezierPath and then use the CGPath accessor to convert it to a CGPath. Unlike the UIGraphics* methods, there are no separate draw* and fill* operations; instead, either the fillColor or strokeColor is set and then the path is filled or stroked (drawn). The UIBezierPath can be constructed by adding segments, but there are several initializers that can be used to draw specific shapes. For example, circles can be drawn with the ovalInRect initializer:

```
func updateUI() {
  let rect = self.bounds
  circle.path = UIBezierPath(ovalInRect: rect).CGPath
}
```

Now when the application is run, a small black circle will be seen on the layers tab:

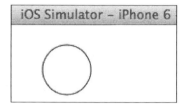

Adding the stop square

The stop square can be added by creating another layer. This will allow the stop button to be turned on or off as necessary. (For example, during a download, the stop button can be shown, and when the download is completed, it can be animated away.)

Add a new constant called square of type CAShapeLayer. It will help to create a constant black as well, since it will be used again elsewhere in the class:

```
class ProgressView: UIView {
  let circle = CAShapeLayer()
  let square = CAShapeLayer()
  let black = UIColor.blackColor().CGColor
}
```

The setupUI method can now be updated to deal with additional layers. Since it is common to set them up in the same way, using a loop is a quick way to set up multiple layers:

```
func setupUI() {
   for layer in [square, circle] {
      layer.strokeColor = black
      layer.fillColor = nil
      self.layer.addSublayer(layer)
   }
   updateUI()
}
```

The path for the square can be created using the rect initializer of UIBezierPath. To create a rectangle that will be centered inside the circle, use the rectByInsetting method with an appropriate value:

```
func updateUI() {
   let rect = self.bounds
   let sq = rect.rectByInsetting(
      dx: rect.width/3, dy: rect.height/3)
   square.fillColor = black
   square.path = UIBezierPath(rect: sq).CGPath
   circle.path = UIBezierPath(ovalInRect: rect).CGPath
}
```

Now when the application is run, the following will be seen:

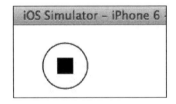

Adding a progress bar

The progress bar can be drawn as an arc representing the amount of data downloaded so far. On other iOS applications, the progress bar starts at the 12 o'clock position and then moves clockwise.

There are two ways to achieve this: using an `arc` that is drawn up to some particular amount, or by setting a single path that represents the entire circle and then using `strokeStart` and `strokeEnd` to define which segment of the path should be drawn. The advantage of using `strokeStart` and `strokeEnd` is that they are **animatable properties**, which allow some animated effects.

The arc needs to be drawn from the top, moved clockwise to the right, and then back up again. The `strokeStart` and `strokeEnd` are `CGFloat` values between 0 and 1, so these can be used to represent the progress of the download.

Easy as Pi

Although circles are often split into 360 degrees (mainly because 360 has a lot of factors and is easily divisible into different numbers), computers tend to work in **radians**. There are 2pi radians in a circle; so half a circle is `pi`, and a quarter of a circle is `pi/2`.

There is a `UIBezierPath` convenience initializer that can draw an arc; the `center` and `radius` are specified along with a `startAngle` and `endAngle` point. The start and end point are both specified in radians, with 0 being the 3 o'clock position and going clockwise or anticlockwise as specified.

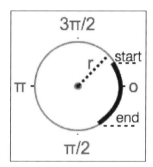

To draw progress starting from the top of the circle, the start point must be specified as `-pi/2`. Drawing clockwise from here around the complete circle takes it to `-pi/2 + 2pi`, which is `3 * pi/2`.

Computers use pi a lot, defined in `usr/include/math.h`, which is included transitively from `UIKit` through the `Darwin` module. The constants `M_PI`, `M_PI_2` (pi/2) and `M_PI_4` (pi/4) and the inverses `M_1_PI` (1/pi) and `M_2_PI` (2/pi) are available.

The middle of the diagram can be calculated by accessing self.center, and the radius of the circle will be half the minimum width or height. To add the path, create a new CAShapeLayer called progress, and optionally give it a different width and color to distinguish it from the background:

```
class ProgressView: UIView {
  let progress = CAShapeLayer()
  var progressAmount: CGFloat = 0.5
  ...
  func setupUI() {
    for layer in [progress, square, circle] {
      ...
    }
    progress.lineWidth = 10
    progress.strokeColor = UIColor.redColor().CGColor
    updateUI()
  }
  func updateUI() {
    ...
    let radius = min(rect.width, rect.height) / 2
    let center = CGPoint(x:rect.midX, y:rect.midY)
    progress.path = UIBezierPath(
      arcCenter: center,
      radius: radius,
      startAngle: CGFloat(-M_PI_2),
      endAngle: CGFloat(3*M_PI_2),
      clockwise: true
    ).CGPath
    progress.strokeStart = 0
    progress.strokeEnd = progressAmount
  }
}
```

When this is run, the progress bar will be seen behind the circle:

Clipping the view

The problem with the progress line is that it extends beyond the circular boundary of the progress view. A simple approach might be to try and calculate a half-width distance from the radius and redraw the circle, but this is fragile as changes to the line width might result in the diagram not looking right in the future.

A better approach is to **mask** the graphics area so that the drawing does not go outside a particular shape. By specifying a mask, any drawing that occurs within the mask is shown; graphics that are drawn outside the mask are not shown.

A mask can be defined as a rectangular area or the result of a filled layer. Creating a circular mask requires creating a new mask layer and then setting a circular path as before.

 A mask can only be used by a single layer. If the same mask is needed for more than one layer, either the mask layer needs to be copied or the mask can be set on a common parent layer.

Create a new `CAShapeLayer` that can be used for the `mask`, and create a `path` based on the `UIBezierPath` with an `ovalInRect`. The `mask` can then be assigned to the `mask` layer of the `progress` layer:

```
class ProgressView: UIView {
  let mask = CAShapeLayer()
  func updateUI() {
    ...
    mask.path = UIBezierPath(ovalInRect:rect).CGPath
    progress.mask = mask
  }
}
```

Now when the display is shown, the progress bar does not bleed over the edge:

Testing views in Xcode

To test the view in interface builder directly, the class can be marked as `@IBDesignable`. This gives permission for Xcode to instantiate and run the view as well as update it for any changes that are made. If the class is marked as `@IBDesignable`, then Xcode will attempt to load the view and display it in storyboard and `xib` files.

However, when the class loads the UI will not be displayed properly, because the frame size needs to be initialized correctly. Override the `layoutSubviews` method to call `updateUI`, which ensures that the view is properly redrawn when the view changes size or is shown for the first time:

```
@IBDesignable class ProgressView: UIView {
  ...
  override func layoutSubviews() {
    setupUI()
  }
}
```

Now when the `ProgressView` is added or shown in interface builder, it will be rendered in place. Build the project, then open the `Main.storyboard`, and click on the progress view; after a brief delay, it will be drawn.

Xcode can also be used to edit different attributes of an object in interface builder. This allows the view to be tested without running the application.

To allow interface builder to edit properties, they can be marked as `@IBInspectable`:

```
@IBDesignable class ProgressView: UIView {
  @IBInspectable var progressAmount: CGFloat = 0.5
  ...
}
```

After building the project, open the storyboard, select the **Progress View**, and go to the **Attributes Inspector**. Just above the **View** section will be a **Progress View** section with the **Progress Amount** field based on the @IBInspectable field of the same name.

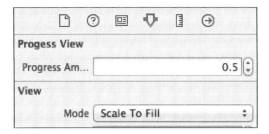

Responding to change

If a UISlider is added to the **Layers View**, changes can be triggered by adding an @IBAction to allow the valueChanged event to propagate the value to the caller.

Create an @IBAction function setProgress, which takes a sender, and then depending on the type of that sender, extract a value:

```
@IBAction func setProgress(sender:AnyObject) {
  switch sender {
    case let slider as UISlider: progressAmount =
      CGFloat(slider.value)
    case let stepper as UIStepper: progressAmount =
      CGFloat(stepper.value)
    default: break
  }
}
```

 Using a switch statement based on the type allows additional views to be added in the future.

The valueChanged event on the UISlider can now be connected to the setProgess on the ProgressView.

Assigning the `progressAmount` value alone has no visible effect, so a property observer can be used to trigger display changes whenever the field is modified. A **property observer** is a block of code that gets called before (`willSet`) or after (`didSet`) a property is changed:

```
@IBInspectable var progressAmount: CGFloat = 0.5 {
  didSet {
    setNeedsLayout()
  }
}
```

Now when the application is run and the slider value is moved, the download amount will be updated in the view. Observe that the changes to the `progressAmount` are animated automatically, so if the slider is quickly moved from one end to the other, the download arc will smoothly animate.

> The property observer uses `setNeedsLayout` to trigger a call to `layoutSubviews` in order to achieve the change in display. Since changes only need to be picked up when a size change occurs or when a property is changed, this is more efficient than implementing other methods such as `drawRect`, which will be called every time the display needs to be updated.

Summary

In this chapter, we looked at several different ways of how to create views in iOS. The first approach was to use interface builder to build the view graphically and some of the problems that this can cause. We then looked at subclassing `UIView` and adding other views to build up a custom view. Finally, we presented two different ways of drawing custom graphics; first with `drawRect` and subsequently with layers.

The next chapter will show how to use networking APIs in iOS to download networked data.

6

Parsing Networked Data

Many iOS applications need to communicate with other servers or devices. This chapter presents both HTTP and non-HTTP networking in Swift and how data can be parsed from either JSON or XML. It first demonstrates how to load data efficiently from URLs followed by how to stream larger data responses. It then concludes with how to perform both synchronous and asynchronous network requests over protocols other than HTTP.

This chapter will present the following topics:

- Loading data from URLs
- Updating the user interface from a background thread
- Parsing JSON and XML data
- Stream-based connections
- Asynchronous data communication

Loading data from URLs

The most common way to load data from a remote network source is to use an HTTP (or HTTPS) URL of the form `https://raw.githubusercontent.com/alblue/com.packtpub.swift.essentials/master/CustomViews/CustomViews/SampleTable.json`.

URLs can be manipulated with the `NSURL` class, which comes from the `Foundation` module (which is transitively imported from the `UIKit` module). The main `NSURL` initializer takes a `String` initializer with a full URL, although other initializers exist for creating relative URLs or for references to file paths.

The NSURLSession class is typically used to perform operations with URLs, and individual sessions can be created through the initializer or the standard **shared session** can be used.

 The NSURLConnection class was used in older versions of iOS and Mac OS X. References to this class might still be seen in some tutorials, or might be required if Mac OS X 10.8 or iOS 6 needs to be supported; otherwise, the NSURLSession class should be preferred.

The NSURLSession class provides a means to create **tasks**. These include:

- **Data task**: This can be used to process network data programmatically
- **Upload task**: This can be used to upload data to a remote server
- **Download task**: This can be used to download to a local storage or to resume a previous or partial download

Tasks are created from the NSURLSession class methods and can take a URL argument and an optional **completion handler**. A completion handler is a lot like a delegate, except that it can be customized per task, and is usually represented as a function.

Tasks can be **suspended** or **resumed** to stop and start the process. Tasks are created in a suspended state by default, so they have to be initially resumed to start processing.

When a data task is completed, the completion handler is called back with three arguments: an NSData object, which represents the returned data; an NSURLResponse object, which represents the response from the remote URL server; and an optional NSError object if anything failed during the request.

With this in place, the SampleTable created in the previous chapter can load data from a network URL by obtaining a session, initiating a data task, and then resuming it. The completion handler will be called when the data is available, which can be used to add the content to the table.

Modify the viewDidLoad method of the SampleTable class to load the SampleTable.json file as follows:

```
let url = NSURL(string: "https://raw.githubusercontent.com/
    alblue/com.packtpub.swift.essentials/master/
    CustomViews/CustomViews/SampleTable.json")!
let session = NSURLSession.sharedSession()
let encoding = NSUTF8StringEncoding
let task = session.dataTaskWithURL(url,completionHandler:
```

```
{data,response,error -> Void in
  let contents = String(NSString(data:data,encoding:encoding)!)
  self.items += [(url.absoluteString!,contents)]
  // table data won't reload - needs to be on ui thread
  self.tableView.reloadData()
})
task.resume()
```

This creates an NSURL and an NSURLSession, and then creates a data task and immediately resumes it. After the content is downloaded, the completion handler is called, which passes the data as an NSData object. The NSString initializer is used to decode UTF8 text from the NSData object and is explicitly cast to a String so that it can be added to the items list.

> The NSURLSession class also provides other factory methods, including one that takes a configuration argument that includes options such as whether responses should be cached, whether network connections should go over the cellular network, and whether any cookies or other headers should be sent with the task.

Finally, the item is added to the items and the tableView is reloaded to show the new data. Note that this does not work immediately if it is not run on the main UI thread; the table has to be rotated or moved in order to redraw the display. Running on the UI thread is covered in the *Networking and user interface* section later in this chapter.

Dealing with errors

Errors are a fact of life, especially on mobile devices with intermittent connectivity. The completion handler is called with a third argument, which represents any error raised during the operation. If this is nil then the operation was a success; if not then the localizedDescription property of the error can be used to notify the user.

For testing purposes, if an error is detected add the localizedDescription to the items in the list. Modify the viewDidLoad method as follows:

```
let task = session.dataTaskWithURL(url, completionHandler:
  {data,response,error -> Void in
    if (error == nil) {
      let contents = String(NSString(data: data,encoding:encoding)!)
      self.items += [(url.absoluteString!,contents)]
    } else {
      self.items += [("Error",error.localizedDescription)]
```

```
    }
    // table data won't reload - needs to be on UI thread
    self.tableView.reloadData()
})
```

An error can be simulated using a nonexistent hostname or an unknown protocol in the URL.

Dealing with missing content

Errors are reported if the remote server cannot be contacted, such as when the hostname is incorrect or the server is down. If the server is operational, then an error will not be reported. It is still possible that the file requested is not found or the server experiences an error while serving the request. These are reported with HTTP status codes.

 If an HTTP URL is not found, the server sends back a 404 status code. This can be used by the client to determine whether a different file should be accessed or whether another server should be queried. For example, browsers will often ask the server for a favicon.ico file and use this to display a small logo; if it is missing, then a generic page icon is shown instead. In general, 4xx responses are client errors, while 5xx responses are server errors.

The NSURLResponse object doesn't have the concept of an HTTP status code, because it can be used for any protocol, including ftp. However, if the request used HTTP, then the response is likely to be HTTP and so the request can be cast to an NSURLHttpResponse, which has a statusCode property. This can be used to provide more specific feedback when the file is not found. Modify the code as follows:

```
if (error == nil) {
  let httpResponse = response as NSHTTPURLResponse
  let statusCode = httpResponse.statusCode
  if (statusCode >= 400 && statusCode < 500) {
    self.items += [("Client error \(statusCode)",
    url.absoluteString!)]
  } else if (statusCode >= 500) {
    self.items += [("Server error \(statusCode)",
    url.absoluteString!)]
  } else {
    let contents = String(NSString(data:data,encoding:encoding)!)
    self.items += [(url.absoluteString!,contents)]
  }
} else {...}
```

Now if the server responds but indicates that either the client made a bad request or the server suffered a problem, the user interface will be updated appropriately.

Nested if and switch statements

Sometimes, the error handling logic can get convoluted by handling different cases, particularly if there are different values that need to be tested. In the previous section, both the NSError and HTTP statusCode needed to be checked.

An alternative approach is to use a switch statement with where clauses. These can be used to test multiple different conditions and also show which part of the condition is being tested. Although a switch statement requires a single expression, it is possible to use a **tuple** to group multiple values into a single expression.

Another advantage of using a tuple is that it permits the cases to be matched on types. In the case of networking, some URLs are based on http or https, which means that the response will be of an NSHTTPURLResponse type. However, if the URL is of a different type (such as a file or ftp protocol), then it will be of a different subtype of NSURLResponse. Unconditionally casting to NSHTTPURLResponse with as will fail in these cases and cause a crash.

The tests can be rewritten as a switch block as follows:

```swift
switch (data,response,error) {
  case (_,_,let e) where e != nil:
    self.items += [("Error",error.localizedDescription)]
  case (_,let r as NSHTTPURLResponse,_)
   where r.statusCode >= 400 && r.statusCode < 500:
    self.items += [("Client error \(r.statusCode)",
     url.absoluteString!)]
  // see note below
  case (_,let r as NSHTTPURLResponse,_)
   where r.statusCode >= 500:
    self.items += [("Server error \(r.statusCode)",
      url.absoluteString!)]
  default:
    let contents = String(NSString(data: data,encoding:encoding)!)
    self.items += [(url.absoluteString!,contents)]
}
```

In this example, the default block is used to execute the success condition and the prior case statements are used to match the error conditions that can be seen.

The final `case` statement causes Swift 1.1 in Xcode 6.1 to hang with 100 percent CPU utilization; as a result, it is commented out in the GitHub repository. A future version of Xcode is likely to fix this behavior. This bug occurs because the second and third case statements match the same expression with different `where` clauses.

The `case (_, _, let e) where e != nil` pattern is an example of a conditional pattern match. The underscore, which is called a **wildcard pattern** in Swift (also known as a **hole** in other languages), is something that will match any value. The third parameter, `let e`, is a **value binding pattern** and has the effect of `let e = error` in this case. Finally, the `where` clause adds the test to ensure that this case only occurs when e is not `nil`.

It is possible to use the `error` identifier instead of `let e` in the case statement; using `case (_, _, _) where error != nil` will have the same effect. However, it is a bad practice to capture values outside the `switch` statement for case matching purposes, since if the `error` variable is renamed, then the `case` statement might become invalid. Generally use `let` patterns inside `case` statements to ensure that the correct expression value is being matched.

The second and third cases perform a `let` assignment, a type test, and conversion. When `case (_, let r as NSHTTPURLResponse, _)` is matched, not only is the value of this part in the tuple assigned the constant `r`, but it is also cast to `NSHTTPURLRepsonse`. If the value is not of type `NSHTTPURLResponse`, then the case statement is automatically skipped. This is equivalent to an `if` test with an `is` expression, followed by a cast with `as`.

Although the patterns are the same in both, the `where` clauses are different. The first `where` clause looks for the case where `r.statusCode` is `400` or greater and less than `500`, while the second is matched where `r.statusCode` is `500` or greater. (Note that as described ealier, the duplicate `case` causes an infinite loop in the Swift compiler for Xcode Version 6.1.)

Regardless of whether nested `if` statements or the `switch` statement is used, the code that performs the test is likely to be very similar. It typically comes down to developer preference, but more developers are likely to be familiar with nested `if` statements. In Swift, the `switch` statement is more powerful than in other languages, so this kind of pattern is likely to become more popular.

Networking and user interfaces

One outstanding problem with the current callback approach is that the callback cannot be guaranteed to be called from the **main thread**. As a result, user interface operations might not work correctly or might throw errors. The right solution is to set up another call using the main thread.

Accessing the main thread in Swift is done in the same way as in Objective-C: using **Grand Central Dispatch** or **GCD**. The **main queue** can be accessed with `dispatch_get_main_queue`, which is used by the thread that all UI updates should occur on. Background tasks are submitted with `dispatch_async` to a queue. To invoke the `reloadData` call on the main thread, wrap it as follows:

```
dispatch_async(dispatch_get_main_queue(), {
    self.tableView.reloadData()})
```

This style of call will be valid for both Objective-C and Swift (although Objective-C uses the ^ (caret) as a block prefix). However, Swift has a special syntax to deal with functions that take blocks; the block can be promoted out of the function's argument and left as a trailing argument. This is known as a **trailing closure**:

```
dispatch_async(dispatch_get_main_queue()) {
    self.tableView.reloadData()
}
```

Although this is a minor difference, it makes it look like `dispatch_async` is more like a keyword such as `if` or `switch` which takes a block of code. This can be used for any function whose final argument is a function; there is no special syntax needed in the function definition. Additionally, the same technique works for functions defined outside of Swift; in the case of `dispatch_async`, the function is defined as a C language function and can be transparently used in a portable way.

Running functions on the main thread

Whenever the UI needs to be updated, the update must be run on the main thread. This can be done using the previous pattern to perform updates, since they will always be threaded. However, it can be a pain to remember to do this each time it is required.

It is possible to build a Swift function that takes another function and runs it on the main thread automatically. NSThread.isMainThread can be used to determine whether the current thread is the UI thread or not, so to run a block of code on the main thread, regardless of whether it's on the main thread or not, the following can be used:

```
func runOnUIThread(fn:()->()) {
  if NSThread.isMainThread() {
    fn()
  } else {
    dispatch_async(dispatch_get_main_queue(), fn)
  }
}
```

This allows the code to be submitted to the background thread simply:

```
self.runOnUIThread(self.tableView.reloadData)
```

Note that due to the lack of parenthesis, the reloadData function is not called, but it is passed in as a function pointer. It is dispatched to the correct thread inside the runOnUIThread function.

If there is more than one function that needs to be called, an inline block can be created. Since this can be passed as a trailing closure to the runOnUIThread method, the parenthesis are optional:

```
self.runOnUIThread {
  self.tableView.backgroundColor = UIColor.redColor()
  self.tableView.reloadData()
  self.tableView.backgroundColor = UIColor.greenColor()
}
```

Parsing JSON

The most popular mechanism to send structured data over a network is to encode it in **JSON**, which stands for **JavaScript Object Notation**. This provides a hierarchical tree data structure that can store simple numeric, logical, and string-based types along with the array and dictionary representations.

Both Mac OS X and iOS come with a built-in parser for JSON documents, in the NSJSONSerialization class. This provides a means to parse a data object and return an NSDictionary that contains the key/value pairs of a JSON object or an NSArray to represent JSON arrays. Other literals are parsed and represented as the NSNumber or NSString values.

The JSON parser uses JSONObjectWithData to create an object from an NSData object containing a string. This is typically the format returned by network APIs and can be created from an existing string using dataUsingEncoding with one of the built-in encoding types, such as NSUTF8StringEncoding.

A simple JSON array of numbers can be parsed as follows:

```
let array = "[1,2,3]".dataUsingEncoding(NSUTF8StringEncoding)!
let parsed = NSJSONSerialization.JSONObjectWithData(
  data:array, options:nil, error:nil)
```

The return type of this is an optional AnyObject. The optionality represents the fact that the data content might not be valid JSON data. It can be cast to an appropriate type using the as keyword; if there is a parsing failure, then an error will be thrown.

The options can be used to indicate whether the return type should be mutable or not. Mutable data allows the caller to add or delete items after being returned from the parsing function; if not specified, the return value will be immutable. The NSJSONReadingOptions options include MutableContainers (containing data structures that are mutable), MutableLeaves (the child leaves are mutable), and AllowFragments (allow non-object, nonarray values to be parsed). Since these are bit flags, they can be combined with | (the bitwise or operator). For example, to specify that both the containers and leaves should be mutable, .MutableContents|.MutableLeaves should be used as the options value.

The SampleTable.json file (referred to in the viewDidLoad method) stores an array of entries, with the title and content fields holding text data per entry:

```
[{"title":"Sample Title","content":"Sample Content"}]
```

To parse the JSON file and entries to the table, replace the default clause in SampleTable with the following:

```
default:
  let parsed = NSJSONSerialization.JSONObjectWithData(
    data, options:nil, error:nil) as NSArray!
  for entry in parsed {
    self.items +=
```

```
    [(entry["title"] as String,
      entry["content"] as String)]
}
```

Running the application will show the **Sample Title** and **Sample Content** entries in the table, which have been loaded and parsed from the book's GitHub repository.

Handling errors

If there are problems parsing the JSON data, then the return type of the JSONObjectWithData function will return a `nil` value. If the type is implicitly unwrapped then accessing the element will cause an error.

The `error` is known as an **inout** argument; by passing a reference to an optional NSError value, the function can assign an instance in addition to the normal return value:

```
var error:NSError? = nil
if let parsed = NSJSONSerialization.JSONObjectWithData(data,
 options:nil, error:&error) {
  // do something with parsed
} else {
  self.items += [("Error",
   "Cannot parse JSON \(error!.localizedDescription)")]
  // show message to user
}
```

The optional `error` is passed into the function with an & (ampersand) symbol. In C, this is used to pass the address of an object, but in Swift, this is limited to inout function parameters. It's mainly used for interoperability with existing C or Objective-C functions; generally using Option to indicate errors is the preferred way in Swift. When the function returns, the `error` will be not `nil` if parsed is `nil` and vice versa.

> Since the `error` is declared an optional value, it must be forcefully unwrapped when being processed in the `else` clause. This is done with `error!` in the string literal that calculates `localizedDescription`.

The `parsed` value will be of the type `AnyObject?`, although the `let` block will implicitly unwrap the value, known as **optional binding**. In the previous section, the code was cast to an `NSArray` directly, but if the returned result is of a different type (for example, an `NSDictionary` or one of the fragment types such as `NSNumber` or `NSString`), then casting to an incorrect type will cause a failure.

The type of the object can be tested with `if [object] is [type]`. However, since the next step is usually to cast it to a different class with `as`, an `as?` shorthand form can perform both the test and the cast in one step:

```
if let array = parsed as? NSArray {
  for entry in array {
    // process elements
  }
} else {
  self.items += [("Error", "JSON is not an array")]
}
```

A `switch` statement can be used to check the type of multiple values at the same time. Since the values are optional `NSString` objects, they need to be converted to a `String` before they can be used in Swift:

```
for entry in array {
  switch (entry["title"], entry["content"]) {
    case (let title as String, let content as String):
      self.items += [(title,content)]
    default:
      self.items += [("Error", "Missing unknown entry")]
  }
}
```

Now when the application is run, errors are detected and handled without the application crashing.

Parsing XML

Although JSON is more commonly used, there are still many XML-based network services. Fortunately, XML parsing has existed in iOS since version 5 in the `NSXMLParser` class and is simple to access from Swift. For example, some data feeds (such as blog posts) use XML documents such as Atom or RSS.

The NSXMLParser is a stream-oriented parser; that is, it reports individual elements as they are seen. The parser calls the delegate to notify when the elements are seen and have finished. When an element is seen, the parser also includes any attributes that were present; for text nodes, it includes the string content.

Thus, the parsing of an XML file involves some state management in the parser. The example used in this section will parse an Atom (news feed) file, whose (simplified) structure looks as follows:

```
<feed xmlns="http://www.w3.org/2005/Atom">
  <title>AlBlue's Blog</title>
  <link href="http://alblue.bandlem.com/atom.xml" rel="self"/>
  <entry>
    <title type="html">Swift - classes></title>
    <link href="http://alblue.bandlem.com/2014/10/swift-classes-
overview.html"/>
    ...
  </entry>
  ...
</feed>
```

In this case, the goal is to extract all the entry elements from the feed; specifically the title and link. This presents a few challenges that will become apparent later on.

Creating a parser delegate

Parsing an XML file requires creating a class that conforms to the NSXMLParserDelegate protocol. To do this, create a new class, FeedParser, that extends NSObject and conforms to the NSXMLParserDelegate protocol.

It should have an init method that takes an NSData and an items property that will be used to acquire the results after they have been parsed:

```
class FeedParser: NSObject, NSXMLParserDelegate {
  var items:[(String,String)] = []
  init(_ data:NSData) {
    // parse XML
  }
}
```

The NSXMLParserDelegate class requires the object to also conform to NSObjectProtocol. The easiest way to do this is to subclass NSObject. Note that the first mentioned supertype is the superclass; the second and subsequent supertypes must be protocols.

Downloading the data

The XML parser can either parse a stream of data as it is downloaded or it can take an NSData object that has been downloaded previously. On successful download, the FeedParser can be used to parse the NSData instance and return a list of items.

Although individual expressions can be assigned temporary values similar to the last time, the statement can be written in a single line (although note that error handling is not present). Add the following to the end of the viewDidLoad method of SimpleTable:

```
session.dataTaskWithURL(
    NSURL(string:"http://alblue.bandlem.com/Tag/swift/atom.xml")!,
    completionHandler: {data,response,error -> Void in
        if data != nil {
            self.items += FeedParser(data).items
            self.runOnUIThread(self.tableView.reloadData)
        }
}).resume()
```

This will download the Atom XML feed for the Swift posts from the author's blog at http://alblue.bandlem.com. Currently, the data is not parsed, so nothing will be added to the table in this step.

> Make sure that both the download operation and the parsing are handled off the main thread, as both of these operations might take some time. Once the data is downloaded it can be parsed, and after it is parsed the UI can be notified to redisplay the contents.

Parsing the data

To process the downloaded XML file, it is necessary to parse the data. This involves writing a parser delegate to listen for the title and link elements. However, the title and link elements exist both at the individual entry level and also at the top level of the blog. Therefore, it is necessary to represent some kind of state in the parser, which detects when the parser is inside an entry element to allow the correct values to be used.

Elements are reported with the `parser:didStartElement:` method and the `parser:didEndElement:` method. This can be used to determine whether the parser is inside an `entry` element by setting a boolean value when an `entry` element starts and resetting it when the `entry` element ends. Add the following to the `FeedParser` class:

```
var inEntry:Bool = false
func parser(parser: NSXMLParser,
  didStartElement elementName: String,
  namespaceURI: String!, qualifiedName:
  String!, attributes: NSDictionary!) {
  switch elementName {
    case "entry":
      inEntry = true
    default: break
  }
}
```

The values of the namespaceURI, qualifiedName, and attributes might be nil. If they are not declared as implicitly unwrapped optionals, then the parser will fail with an EXC_BAD_ACCESS when calling the parse method.

The `link` stores the value of the references in an `href` attribute of the element. This is passed when the start element is called, so is trivial to store. At this point, the `title` might not be known, so the value of the `link` has to be stored in an optional field:

```
var link:String?
...
// in parser:didStartElement method
case "entry":
  inEntry = true
case "link":
  link = attributes.objectForKey("href") as String?
default break;
```

The `title` stores its data as a text node, which needs to be implemented with another boolean flag, indicating whether the parser is inside a `title` node. Text nodes are reported with the `parser:foundCharacters:` delegate method. Add the following to the `FeedParser`:

```
var title:String?
var inTitle: Bool = false
...
// in parser:didStartElement method
case "entry":
  inEntry = true
case "title":
  inTitle = true
case "link":
...
func parser(parser: NSXMLParser, foundCharacters string:String) {
  if inEntry && inTitle {
    title = string
  }
}
```

By storing the `title` and `link` as optional fields, when the end of the `entry` element is seen, the fields can be appended into the `items` list, followed by resetting the state of the parser:

```
func parser(parser: NSXMLParser,
 didEndElement elementName: String,
 namespaceURI: String!, qualifiedName: String!) {
  switch elementName {
    case "entry":
      inEntry = false
      if title != nil && link != nil {
        items += [(title!,link!)]
      }
      title = nil
      link = nil
    case "title":
      inTitle = false
    default: break
  }
}
```

Finally, having implemented the callback methods, the remaining steps are to create an NSXMLParser from the data passed in previously, set the delegate (and optionally the namespace handling), and then to invoke the parser:

```
init(_ data:NSData) {
  let parser = NSXMLParser(data: data)
  parser.shouldProcessNamespaces = true
  super.init()
  parser.delegate = self
  parser.parse()
}
```

 Note that the assignment of self to the delegate cannot be done until after the super.init has been called.

Now when the application is run, a set of news feed items will be displayed.

Direct network connections

Although most application networking will involve downloading content over standard protocols such as HTTP(S) and using standard representations, there are times when having a specific data stream protocol is required. In this case, a **stream** oriented process will allow individual bytes to be read or written, or a **datagram** or **packet** oriented process can be used to send individual packets of data.

There are networking libraries to support both; an NSStream higher-level Objective-C based class provides the mechanism to drive stream-based responses, and although lower-level packet connections are possible with the CoreFoundation or the POSIX layer, local multiplayer gaming using the MultipeerConnectivity module is often appropriate.

 Local networking with the MultipeerConnectivity module involves creating an MCSession, followed by sendData to send NSData objects to connected peers and using the MCSessionDelegate to receiveData from connected peers. This is often used to synchronize the state of the world, such as the player's current location or health.

Opening a stream connection

A stream is a reliable, ordered sequence of bytes, which is used by most internet protocols. Streams can be created from a network host and port using the `NSStream` class method `getStreamsToHostWithName`, added in iOS 8 and part of Mac OS X. This allows an `NSInputStream` and `NSOutputStream` to be acquired at the same time.

 Since this is an existing Objective-C API, the streams are returned via inout parameters. In Swift, this translates to the parameters being passed back with an ampersand (`&`) and declaring the variables as optional.

The input and output streams can then be used to send data asynchronously or synchronously. Asynchronous mechanisms involve scheduling the data processing on the application's run-loop and is covered in the *Asynchronous reading and writing* section. Synchronous mechanisms use `read` and `write` to receive or send buffers of data.

 Once the streams have been acquired, they need to be **open** in order to receive or send data. Forgetting this step will result in, no networking data being sent.

To simplify the process of acquiring streams, the following can be created as an **extension** of the `NSStream` class. An extension makes a method appear to come from an original class but is implemented externally to that class. Add the following `StreamExtensions.swift` file to the `CustomViews` project with the following content:

```swift
extension NSStream {
  class func open(host:String,_ port:Int)
    -> (NSInputStream, NSOutputStream)? {
    var input:NSInputStream?
    var output:NSOutputStream?
    NSStream.getStreamsToHostWithName(
      host, port: port,
      inputStream: &input,
      outputStream: &output)
    if input == nil || output == nil {
      return nil
    } else {
      output!.open()
```

```
            input!.open()
            return (input!,output!)
        }
    }
}
```

A connection to a remote host can be obtained by calling `NSStream.`
`open(host,port)`, which returns an open pair of input/output streams.

Synchronous reading and writing

The `NSInputStream` method `read` allows bytes to be read from a stream
synchronously, while the `NSOutputStream` method `write` allows bytes to be written
to a stream. These take different types, but the most common approach is to create an
array of bytes `[UInt8]` in Swift as the buffer, and then read into it or from it with an
`UnsafeMutablePointer` (equivalent to an ampersand in C).

The `read` and `write` methods both return a number of bytes read/written. This
can be negative (in the case of an error), zero, or positive in the case of bytes having
been processed. Both calls take a buffer and a maximum length, though it is not
guaranteed that the full maximum length will be processed.

> Always check the return value of `write` or `read`, since it is possible that
> only part of the buffer has been written. A best practice (for synchronous
> connections) is to wrap the call in a `while` loop or have some other form
> of retry in order to ensure that all the data is written.

Writing data to an NSOutputStream

To make it easier to write `NSData` content to streams, an extension method on
`NSOutputStream` can be created that performs a full write, based on the size of
the data:

```
extension NSOutputStream {
    func writeData(data:NSData) -> Int {
        let size = data.length
        var completed = 0
        while completed < size {
            var wrote = write(UnsafePointer(data.bytes) +
            completed, maxLength:size - completed)
            if wrote < 0 {
                return wrote
```

```
      } else {
        completed += wrote
      }
    }
    return completed
  }
}
```

The code takes an `NSData` and writes it to the underlying stream, returning the number of bytes written (or a negative value if there are problems). The return value of the `write` method is checked, and if the value is negative, returned to the caller directly. Otherwise, the `completed` counter is incremented with the number of bytes written.

If the number of written bytes reaches the size of the data requested, then the value is returned. Otherwise the loop recurs, this time starting at the point it left off.

 Although uncommon in Swift, pointer arithmetic is possible by acquiring `UnsafePointer` to the `data.bytes` array and then incrementing by the number of bytes already written. The length of the remaining bytes is calculated with `size-completed`.

Reading from an NSInputStream

A similar approach can be used to read a full buffer from an `NSInputStream` by creating a `readBytes` method that returns an array of bytes of a known size and a means to convert this to an `NSData` for easier processing/parsing:

```
extension NSInputStream {
  func readBytes(size:Int) -> [UInt8]? {
    let buffer = Array<UInt8>(count:size,repeatedValue:0)
    var completed = 0
    while completed < size {
      let read = self.read(
       UnsafeMutablePointer(buffer) + completed,
       maxLength: size - completed)
      if read < 0 {
        return nil
      } else {
        completed += read
      }
    }
    return buffer
```

```
    }
    func readData(size:Int) -> NSData? {
      if let buffer = readBytes(size) {
        return NSData(
          bytes: UnsafeMutablePointer(buffer),
          length: buffer.count)
      } else {
        return nil
      }
    }
  }
```

The readData method returns an NSData, while the readBytes method returns an array of UInt8 values. The NSData approach is useful in some cases (particularly, for creating a String from the returned data), and in other cases being able to process the bytes directly is useful (for example, parsing binary formats). Having both allows either of these to be used as appropriate.

 Synchronous reads can block forever; if the client application requests exactly 10 bytes but the server only sends 9 bytes, then it will hang permanently until the tenth byte is sent. It is a better practice to use asynchronous reads, which cannot block in this way.

Reading and writing hexadecimal and UTF8 data

Being able to process data as UTF8 values or hexadecimal values can be useful in some protocols. Although both NSString and NSData provide means to convert to and from UTF8, the syntax is overly verbose, as it is based on preexisting Objective-C methods.

To facilitate the conversions, extension methods can be created to provide a simple way of converting to and from UTF8 representations. In addition to class and instance functions, it is possible to use extensions to add dynamic properties to an existing object. This can be used to create the utf8data and utf8string properties on NSData and String by adding extensions in a file Extensions.swift as follows:

```
extension NSData {
  var utf8string:String {
    return NSString(data:self,
      encoding:NSUTF8StringEncoding)!
  }
}
extension String {
```

```
    var utf8data:NSData {
      return self.dataUsingEncoding(
        NSUTF8StringEncoding, allowLossyConversion: false)!
    }
  }
```

This allows expressions such as `data.utf8string` and `string.utf8data`, which are much more compact. Each time the expression is evaluated, the associated getter function will be called.

> There is no standard convention for naming extensions in Swift at the time this book was written. If there are extensions to a single type of data—such as the streams previously—then the file can be named `[Type]Extensions.swift`. Alternatively, the name can be used for the type of methods called; for example, in this case `UTF8Extensions.swift` could have been used.

Parsing hexadecimal data from strings and integers can also be added to the `String` and `Int` types, as follows:

```
extension String {
  func fromHex() -> Int {
    var result = 0
    for c in self {
      result *= 16
      switch c {
      case "0":result += 0      case "1":result += 1
      case "2":result += 2      case "3":result += 3
      case "4":result += 4      case "5":result += 5
      case "6":result += 6      case "7":result += 7
      case "8":result += 8      case "9":result += 9
      case "a","A":result += 10 case "b","B":result += 11
      case "c","C":result += 12 case "d","D":result += 13
      case "e","E":result += 14 case "f","F":result += 15
      default: break
      }
    }
    return result;
  }
}
extension Int {
```

```
    func toHex(digits:Int) -> String {
      return NSString(format:"%0\(digits)x",self)
    }
  }
}
```

This allows hex values to be created with `int.toHex` and `string.fromHex`.

Implementing the git protocol

It is possible to write a client to query a remote git server using the `git://` protocol to determine the hashes of remote tags/branches/references.

> The `git://` protocol works by sending **packet lines** of data, with each line prefixed with four hexadecimal digits in ASCII, indicating the length of the rest of the data (including the four initial digits). Sending a `git-upload-pack` request will return a list of references on the remote repository.

Since the `git://` protocol uses packet lines, create a `PacketLineExtensions.swift` file with the following content:

```
extension NSOutputStream {
  func writePacketLine(_ message:String = "") -> Int {
    let data = message.utf8data
    let length = data.length
    if length == 0 {
      return writeData("0000".utf8data)
    } else {
      let prefix = (length + 4).toHex(4).utf8data
      return self.writeData(prefix) + self.writeData(data)
    }
  }
}
```

When an empty `NSData` object is passed, the special packet line `0000` is written, indicating the end of the conversation. When a non-empty `NSData` is written, the length of the data is written as a hexadecimal value (including the 4 bytes for the length) followed by the data itself.

This will result in a protocol conversation like:

```
> 004egit-upload-pack /alblue/com.packtpub.swift.essentials.
git\0host=github.com\0
< 00dfadaa46b98ce211ff819f0bb343395ad6a2ec6ef1 HEAD\0multi_ack
thin-pack side-band side-band-64k ofs-delta shallow no-progress
include-tag multi_ack_detailed symref=HEAD:refs/heads/master
agent=git/2:2.1.1+github-611-gd89bd9f
< 003fadaa46b98ce211ff819f0bb343395ad6a2ec6ef1 refs/heads/master
> 0000
< 0000
```

Reading a packet line is similar:

```
extension NSInputStream {
  func readPacketLine() -> NSData? {
    if let data = readData(4) {
      let length = data.utf8string.fromHex()
      if length == 0 {
        return nil
      } else {
        return readData(length - 4)
      }
    } else {
      return nil
    }
  }
  func readPacketLineString() -> NSString? {
    if let data = self.readPacketLine() {
      return data.utf8string
    } else {
      return nil
    }
  }
}
```

In this case, the first 4 bytes are read to determine what the remaining length is. If it is zero, a `nil` value is returned to indicate the end of the stream. If it is non-zero, the data is read (less the 4 that is used for the packet line length header). An additional `readPacketLineString` is provided to allow an easy creation of the packet line as an `NSString`.

Listing git references remotely

To remotely query a git repository for references, the `git-upload-pack` command needs to be sent, along with a reference to the repository in question and optionally a host as well. To provide an API to query this programmatically, create a `RemoteGitRepository` class with an initializer that stores the host, port, and repository; and a `lsRemote` function, which returns the value of the references:

```
class RemoteGitRepository {
  let host:String
  let repo:String
  let port:Int
  init(host:String, repo:String, _ port:Int = 9418) {
    self.host = host
    self.repo = repo
    self.port = port
  }
  func lsRemote() -> [String:String] {
    var refs = [String:String]()
    // load the data
    return refs
  }
}
```

To load the data from the repository, a connection to the remote host needs to be made on the default port (in this case, `9418` is the default for the `git://` protocol). Once the streams have been opened, the `git-upload-pack [repository]\0host=[host]\0` packet line is sent, and subsequently, lines can be read of the form `hash reference`:

```
if let (input,output) = NSStream.open(host,port) {
  output.writePacketLine(
    "git-upload-pack \(repo)\0host=\(host)\0")
  while true {
    if let response = input.readPacketLineString() {
      let hash = String(response.substringToIndex(41))
      let ref = String(response.substringFromIndex(41))
      if ref.hasPrefix("HEAD") {
        continue
      } else {
        refs[ref] = hash
      }
    } else {
      break
```

```
      }
    }
    output.writePacketLine()
    input.close()
    output.close()
}
```

Calling the `lsRemote` function on a `RemoteGitRepository` instance with an appropriate `host` and `repo` will return a list of hashes by reference.

Integrating the network call into the UI

Since the network can introduce delays or can even result in a complete failure, network calls should never be performed on the UI thread. Previously, the `SampleTable` was used to introduce a `runOnUIThread` function. A similar approach can be used to run a function on a background thread:

```
func runOnBackgroundThread(fn:()->()) {
  dispatch_async(
    dispatch_get_global_queue(
      DISPATCH_QUEUE_PRIORITY_DEFAULT, 0)
    ,fn)
}
```

This will permit `viewDidLoad` to invoke a call in order to query the remote references from the repository and add them to the table. As before, the call to update the table must be called from the UI thread. Add the following to the end of the `viewDidLoad` method:

```
runOnBackgroundThread {
  let repo = RemoteGitRepository(host: "github.com",
   repo: "/alblue/com.packtpub.swift.essentials.git")
  for (ref,hash) in repo.lsRemote() {
    self.items += [(ref,hash)]
  }
  self.runOnUIThread(self.tableView.reloadData)
}
```

Now, when the application is launched, entries corresponding to the branches and tags in the remote repository should be added to the table.

Asynchronous reading and writing

Besides synchronous reading and writing, it is also possible to perform **asynchronous** reading and writing. Instead of spinning in a `while` loop, the application can use callbacks scheduled on the application's **run loop**.

To receive callbacks, a class that implements `NSStreamDelegate` must be created and assigned to the stream's `delegate` field. When events occur, the `stream` method is called, to which the type of event as well as the associated stream are passed.

The stream is registered with `scheduleInRunLoop` (using `NSRunLoop.mainRunLoop()` with a `NSDefaultRunLoopMode` mode). Finally, the stream can be opened.

> If the stream is opened before the delegate is set or scheduled in the `run` loop, then events will not be delivered.

Events are defined in the `NSStreamEvent` class and include `HasSpaceAvailable` (for output streams) and `HasBytesAvailable` (for input streams). By responding to callbacks, the application can process results asynchronously.

> When using Swift, the `NSStreamDelegate` is treated as a `weak` delegate on the input or output stream. This poses problems when using an inline class to provide input parsing; doing so will result in an `EXC_BAD_ACCESS`, as the delegate is automatically reclaimed by the runtime. This can be avoided by storing a strong circular reference to `self` in the initializer and assigning it to `nil` when the streams are closed.

Reading data asynchronously from an NSInputStream

This is especially useful for asynchronous protocols, such as XMPP, which might send additional messages at arbitrary times. It also allows battery-powered devices to not spin the CPU, should the remote server be slow or hang.

To receive data asynchronously, a delegate must implement the `NSStreamDelegate` method `stream(stream:handleEvent)`. When data is available, the `HasBytesAvailable` event will be sent, and data can be read accordingly.

To convert the previous example to an asynchronous form, a few changes need to be made. Firstly, the `open` extension method created in the *Opening a stream connection* section needs to be augmented with a `connect` method, which does not perform the `open` immediately:

```
class func open(host:String,_ port:Int)
 -> (NSInputStream, NSOutputStream)? {
  if let (input,output) = connect(host,port) {
    input.open()
    output.open()
    return (input,output)
  } else {
    return nil
  }
}
class func connect(host:String,_ port:Int)
   -> (NSInputStream, NSOutputStream)? {
… // as before but with open commented out
  // input!.open()
  // output!.open()
…
}
```

> In order to receive events asynchronously, the delegate must be set and the stream must be scheduled on a `run` loop before the stream is opened.

Creating a stream delegate

To create a stream delegate, create a file called `PacketLineParser.swift` with the following content:

```
class PacketLineParser: NSObject, NSStreamDelegate {
  let output:NSOutputStream
  let callback:(NSString)->()
  var capture:PacketLineParser?
  init(_ output:NSOutputStream, _ callback:(NSString) -> ()) {
    self.output = output
    self.callback = callback
    super.init()
    capture = self
  }
  func stream(stream: NSStream, handleEvent: NSStreamEvent) {
```

```
        let input = stream as NSInputStream
        if handleEvent == NSStreamEvent.HasBytesAvailable {
          if let line = input.readPacketLineString() {
            callback(line)
          } else {
            output.writePacketLine()
            input.close()
            output.close()
            capture = nil
          }
        }
      }
    }
```

This parser has a callback that is invoked for each packet line read; when the HasBytesAvailable event is sent, the line is read (using the same synchronous mechanism as before) and then passed to the callback. Unlike the synchronous approach, there is no while loop here—when data is available, it triggers the parsing of the data.

> Since this will be assigned to an input stream delegate (which holds a weak reference), it is necessary to capture a cyclic reference to itself with capture = self in order to avoid the runtime from evicting the instance. When the streams are closed, the capture will be set to nil, which will release the instance.

The readPacketLine returns a nil to indicate either an error or a completed stream; in this case, an empty packet line is sent (to tell the remote server that no further interaction is required) and then both the streams are closed.

Dealing with errors

It is necessary to clean up the streams and remove them from run loops, both when the stream content is successful or when communication errors occur. In addition to the HasBytesAvailable event, there are events that are sent when the stream's end is encountered or an error occurs.

These should be handled in the same way as when the connection comes to a natural end; resources should be tidied, and in particular, the streams should be removed from run loop processing. Finally, the cyclic reference should be removed to permit the delegate object to be removed.

The existing `close` code can be moved to its own separate function, and additional cases of the stream ending or errors occurring can perform the same cleanup:

```
func stream(stream: NSStream, handleEvent: NSStreamEvent) {
  let input = stream as NSInputStream
  if handleEvent == NSStreamEvent.HasBytesAvailable {
    if let line = input.readPacketLineString() {
      callback(line)
    } else {
      closeStreams(input,output)
    }
  }
  if handleEvent == NSStreamEvent.EndEncountered
  || handleEvent == NSStreamEvent.ErrorOccurred {
    closeStreams(input,output)
  }
}
func closeStreams(input:NSInputStream,_ output:NSOutputStream) {
  if capture != nil {
    capture = nil
    output.removeFromRunLoop(NSRunLoop.mainRunLoop(),
      forMode: NSDefaultRunLoopMode)
    input.removeFromRunLoop(NSRunLoop.mainRunLoop(),
      forMode: NSDefaultRunLoopMode)
    input.delegate = nil
    output.delegate = nil
    if output.streamStatus != NSStreamStatus.Closed {
      output.writePacketLine()
      output.close()
    }
    if input.streamStatus != NSStreamStatus.Closed {
      input.close()
    }
  }
}
```

Listing references asynchronously

To provide a list of references asynchronously, the delegate has to be set up with a suitable callback that will parse the returned data. Instead of the method returning a dictionary (which would require synchronous blocking), a callback will be passed which can be called with references as they are found.

 Note that there are two separate callbacks: the PacketLineParser callback (which reads in the network data and returns the NSString instances on a per packet line basis) and the reference parsing callback (which translates the NSString into a (String,String) tuple).

To start the process, the git-upload-pack needs to be sent synchronously, after which subsequent responses will be processed asynchronously. This can be done by creating a new method, lsRemoteAsync, which takes a callback function for the (String,String) tuple:

```
func lsRemoteAsync(fn:(String,String) -> ()) {
  if let (input,output) = NSStream.connect(host,port) {
    input.delegate = PacketLineParser(output) {
    (response:NSString) -> () in
      let hash = String(response.substringToIndex(41))
      let ref = String(response.substringFromIndex(41))
      if !ref.hasPrefix("HEAD") {
        fn(ref,hash)
      }
    }
    input.scheduleInRunLoop(NSRunLoop.mainRunLoop(),
     forMode: NSDefaultRunLoopMode)
    input.open()
    output.open()
    output.writePacketLine(
     "git-upload-pack \(repo)\0host=\(host)\0")
  }
}
```

This creates a connection (but without opening the streams), sets the delegate and schedules the run loop for the input stream, and finally opens both the streams for interaction. Once this is done, the initial git-upload-pack message is sent as before. At this point, the lsRemoteAsync method returns, and subsequent events occur when input data is received from the server.

When a line is received through the `PacketLineParser` callback, it is split into a reference and a hash and then hands the results to the callback passed into the argument in the first place.

 Asynchronous programming often involves many callbacks. Instead of a synchronous program that might look like `A;B;C;` an asynchronous program often looks like `A(callback:B(callback:C))`. When an input trigger occurs—a network request, user interaction, or timer firing—a sequence of actions can occur via these nested callbacks.

Asynchronous pipelines are generally preferred for battery performance reasons, as blocking in a `while` spin loop will waste CPU energy until the condition is satisfied.

Displaying asynchronous references in the UI

To display the asynchronous data to the screen, the callback must be modified to allow individual elements to update the GUI.

In `SampleTable`, instead of calling `repo.lsRemote` (which performs a synchronous lookup) use `repo.lsRemoteAsync`. This requires a callback, which can be used to update the table data and can cause the view to reload the contents:

```
// for (ref,hash) in repo.lsRemote() {
//   self.items += [(ref,hash)]
// }
repo.lsRemoteAsync() { (ref:String,hash:String) in
  self.items += [(ref,hash)]
  self.runOnUIThread(self.tableView.reloadData)
}
```

Now when the application is run, the references will be updated asynchronously and the UI will not be blocked by a slow or hung server.

Writing data asynchronously to an NSOutputStream

Asynchronous sending is not as useful as asynchronous reading unless large uploads are required. If there is a lot of data, then it is unlikely to be written synchronously in a single `write` call. It is better to perform any additional writes asynchronously.

To write data asynchronously requires storing the `completed` count as a variable outside the function. The `write` method can be used to replace the `while` loop as before, by writing a segment of the data on each iteration of the stream method. Although code isn't needed in this example, this is how the code could look:

```
...
self.data = data
// initial write to kick off subsequent events
completed = output.write(UnsafePointer(data.bytes),
 maxLength: data.length
...
var completed:Int
var data:NSData?
func stream(stream: NSStream, handleEvent: NSStreamEvent) {
  let output = stream as NSOutputStream
  if handleEvent == NSStreamEvent.HasSpaceAvailable
  && data != nil {
    let size = data!.length
    completed += output.write(
     UnsafePointer(data!.bytes) + completed,
     maxLength: size - completed)
    if completed == size {
      completed = 0
      data = nil
    }
  }
}
```

Asynchronous data always starts with a call to synchronously write the data. If not all of the data is written (in other words, `completed` < `size`), then subsequent callbacks will occur on the `NSStreamDelegate`. This can then pick up where the `data` value left off, using a similar technique to the synchronous case but without a `while` loop. Instead of the iteration blocking to write the whole data value, the stream call will be called multiple times (in effect replacing each iteration of the `while` loop). In the final run, when `completed` == `size`, the data is released and the completion counter is reset.

The stream callback is called enough number of times to write all the data. If no data is written, then events are no longer called. New data is only written when an additional value is passed. Care must be taken when writing data from different threads, since the data value is processed as an instance variable and overwriting it might cause data to be lost. The reader is invited to extend the single element data into an array of outstanding data elements so that they can be queued up appropriately.

Summary

This chapter presented the common techniques to deal with networked data in Swift-based applications, with a particular focus on how to maximize battery usage on portable devices using asynchronous techniques to access data.

Since most network requests are likely to provide either a JSON or XML based representation over HTTP(S), the first section of this chapter covered using NSURLSession and the asynchronous dataTask operations to pull data down from a remote server. The second and third sections then presented how this data can be parsed from either JSON or XML, depending on the format required.

The last section presented how to make network connections directly in order to deal with protocols other than HTTP, and as an example, showed how a remote git command can be executed to find out which references are available in a remote git repository. This was presented in two forms: as a synchronous API (to demonstrate the technique of how to work with streams and to explain the git protocol) followed by its conversion to an asynchronous API. This can be used to minimize CPU cycles and thus battery usage, to allow other such translations to be performed in the future.

The final chapter will present how to integrate all the ideas covered in this book into an iOS application to display GitHub repositories.

7
Building a Repository Browser

Having covered how to integrate the components necessary to build an application, this chapter will create a repository browser that allows user repositories to be displayed using the GitHub API.

This chapter will present the following topics:

- An overview of the GitHub API
- Talking to the GitHub API with Swift
- Creating a repository browser
- Maintaining selection between view controllers

An overview of the GitHub API

The GitHub API provides a REST-based interface using JSON to return information about users and repositories. Version 3 of the API is documented at `https://developer.github.com/v3/` and is the version used in this book.

The API is rate limited; at the time of writing, anonymous requests can be made up to sixty times per hour, while logged in users have a higher limit. The code repository for this book has sample responses that can be used for testing and development purposes.

The root endpoint

The main entry point to GitHub is the **root endpoint**. For the main GitHub site this is `https://api.github.com` and for GitHub Enterprise installations it is `https://hostname.example.org/api/v3/` along with user credentials. The endpoint provides a collection of URLs that can be used to find specific resources:

```
{
  ...
  "issue_search_url": "https://api.github.com/search/issues?q={query}
{&page,per_page,sort,order}",
  "issues_url": "https://api.github.com/issues",
  "repository_url": "https://api.github.com/repos/{owner}/{repo}",
  "user_url": "https://api.github.com/users/{user}",  "user_
repositories_url": "https://api.github.com/users/{user}/
repos{?type,page,per_page,sort}",
  ...}
```

The services are URI templates. Text in braces {} is replaced on demand with the values of parameters; text that starts with `{?a,b,c}` is expanded to form `?a=&b=&c=` if present and missing otherwise. For example, with a user of `alblue`, the `user_url` of the user resource at `https://api.github.com/users/{user}` becomes `https://api.github.com/users/alblue`.

The user resource

The user resource for a specific user contains information about their repositories (`repos_url`), name, and other information, such as a location and blog (if provided). In addition, the `avatar_url` provides a URL to an image which can be used to display the user's avatar. For example, `https://api.github.com/users/alblue` contains:

```
{
  ...
  "login": "alblue",
  "avatar_url": "https://avatars.githubusercontent.com/u/76791?v=2",
  "repos_url": "https://api.github.com/users/alblue/repos",
  "name": "Alex Blewitt",
  "blog": "http://alblue.bandlem.com",
  "location": "Milton Keynes, UK",
  ...
}
```

The `repos_url` link can be used to find the user's repositories. This is the same that is reported at the root endpoint as the `user_repositories_url` with the `{user}` already replaced with the username.

The repositories resource

Repositories for a user can be accessed via the `repos_url` or `user_repositories_url` references. This returns an array of JSON objects containing information such as:

```
[{
  "name": "com.packtpub.e4.swift.essentials",
  "html_url":
    "https://github.com/alblue/com.packtpub.swift.essentials",
  "clone_url":
    "https://github.com/alblue/com.packtpub.swift.essentials.git",
  "description": "Swift Essentials",
},{
  "name": "com.packtpub.e4",
  "html_url":
    "https://github.com/alblue/com.packtpub.e4",
  "clone_url":
    "https://github.com/alblue/com.packtpub.e4.git",
  "description":
    "Eclipse Plugin Development by Example: Beginners Guide",
},{
  "name": "com.packtpub.e4.advanced",
  "html_url":
    "https://github.com/alblue/com.packtpub.e4.advanced",
  "clone_url":
    "https://github.com/alblue/com.packtpub.e4.advanced.git",
  "description":
    "Advanced Eclipse plug-in development",
}...]
```

The RepositoryBrowser project

The client is a **Master Detail** application called `RepositoryBrowser`. This sets up a template that can be used on a large device with a split view controller, or a navigator view controller on a small device. In addition, actions to add entries are created.

To build the APIs necessary to display content, several utility classes are needed:

- The `URITemplate` class processes URI templates with a set of key/value pairs
- The `Threads` class allows functions to be run in the background or in the main thread

- The `NSURLExtensions` class provides easy parsing JSON objects from a URL
- The `DictionaryExtensions` class provides a means of creating a Swift dictionary from a JSON object
- The `GitHubAPI` class provides access to the GitHub remote API

URI templates

URI templates are defined in RFC 6570 at `https://tools.ietf.org/html/rfc6570`. They can be used to replace sequences of text surrounded by { } in a URI. Although GitHub's API uses optional values {?...}, the example client presented in this chapter will not need to use these, and so they can be ignored in this implementation.

The template class replaces the parameters with values from a dictionary. To create the API, it is useful to write a test case first, following test-driven development. A test case class can be created by navigating to **File | New | File... | iOS | Source | Test Case Class** and creating a subclass of `XCTestCase` in Swift. The test code will look like:

```
import XCTest
class URITemplateTests: XCTestCase {
  func testURITemplate() {
    let template = "http://example.com/{blah}/blah/{?blah}"
    let replacement = URITemplate.replace(
     template,values: ["blah":"foo"])
    XCTAssertEqual("http://example.com/foo/blah/",
     replacement,"Template replacement")
  }
}
```

The `replace` function requires string processing. Although the function could be a class function or an extension on `String`, having it as a separate class makes testing easier. The function signature looks like:

```
import Foundation
class URITemplate {
  class func replace(template:String, values:[String:String])
    -> String {
    var replacement = template
    while true {
      // replace until no more {…} are present
    }
    return replacement
  }
}
```

Make sure that the URITemplate class is added to the test target as well; otherwise, the test script will not compile.

The parameters are matched using a regular expression such as { [^}]*}. To search or access this from a string involves a Range of String.Index values. These are like integer indexes into the string, but instead of referring to a character by its byte offset, the index is an abstract representation. (Some character encodings such as UTF-8 use multiple bytes to represent a single character.)

The rangeOfString method takes a string or regular expression and returns a range if there is a match present (or nil if there isn't). This can be used to detect whether a pattern is present, or to break out of the while loop:

```
// replace until no more {…} are present
if let parameterRange = replacement.rangeOfString(
  "\\{[^}]*\\}",
  options: NSStringCompareOptions.RegularExpressionSearch) {
  // perform a replacement of parameterRange
} else {
  break
}
```

The parameterRange contains a start and end index that represent the locations of the { and } characters. The value of the parameter can be extracted with replacement.substringWithRange(parameterRange). If it starts with {?, it is replaced with an empty string:

```
// perform a replacement of parameterRange
var value:String
let parameter = replacement.substringWithRange(parameterRange)
if parameter.hasPrefix("{?") {
  value = ""
} else {
  // substitute with real replacement
}
replacement.replaceRange(parameterRange, with: value)
```

Finally, if the replacement is of the form {user}, then the value of user is acquired from the dictionary and used as the replacement value. To get the name of the parameter, startIndex has to be advanced to the successor, and endIndex has to be reversed to the predecessor to account for the { and } characters:

```
// substitute with real replacement
let start = parameterRange.startIndex.successor()
let end = parameterRange.endIndex.predecessor()
let name = replacement.substringWithRange(
  Range<String.Index>(start:start,end:end))
value = values[name] ?? ""
```

Now, when the test is run by navigating to **Product** | **Test** or by pressing *Command +* *U*, the string replacement will pass.

 The ?? is an optional test that is used to return the first argument, if it is present, and the second argument, if it is nil.

Background threading

Background threading allows functions to be trivially launched on the UI thread or on a background thread, as appropriate. This was explained in *Chapter 6, Parsing Networked Data*, in the *Networking and user interface* section. Add the following as Threads.swift:

```
import Foundation
class Threads {
  class func runOnBackgroundThread(fn:()->()) {
    dispatch_async(dispatch_get_global_queue(
      DISPATCH_QUEUE_PRIORITY_DEFAULT, 0),fn)
  }
  class func runOnUIThread(fn:()->()) {
    if(NSThread.isMainThread()) {
      fn()
    } else {
      dispatch_async(dispatch_get_main_queue(), fn)
    }
  }
}
```

The `Threads` class can be tested with the following test case:

```
import XCTest
class ThreadsTest: XCTestCase {
  func testThreads() {
    Threads.runOnBackgroundThread {
      XCTAssertFalse(NSThread.isMainThread(),
       "Running on background thread")
      Threads.runOnUIThread {
        XCTAssertTrue(NSThread.isMainThread(),
          "Running on UI thread")
      }
    }
  }
}
```

When the tests are run by pressing *Command + U*, the tests should pass.

Parsing JSON dictionaries

As many network responses are returned in JSON format, and to make JSON parsing easier, extensions can be added to the NSURL class to facilitate acquiring and parsing of content loaded from network locations. Instead of designing a synchronous extension that blocks until data is available, using a callback function is better practice. Create a file named NSURLExtensions.swift with the following content:

```
extension NSURL {
  func withJSONDictionary(fn:[String:String] -> ()) {
    let session = NSURLSession.sharedSession()
    session.dataTaskWithURL(self) {
      data,response,error -> () in
      if let json = NSJSONSerialization.JSONObjectWithData(
        data, options: nil, error: nil) as? [String:AnyObject] {
        // fn(json)
      } else {
        fn([String:String]())
      }
    }.resume()
  }
}
```

This provides an extension for an NSURL to provide a JSON dictionary. However, the data type returned from the JSONObjectWithData method is [String:AnyObject], not [String:String]. Although it might be expected that it could just be cast to the right type, the as will perform a test and if there are mixed values (such as a number or nil) then the entire object is considered invalid. Instead, the JSON data structure must be converted to a [String:String] type. Add the following as a standalone function to NSURLExtensions.swift:

```
func toStringString(dict:[String:AnyObject]) -> [String:String] {
  var result:[String:String] = [:]
  for (key,value) in dict {
    if let valueString = value as? String {
      result[key] = valueString
    } else {
      result[key] = "\(value)"
    }
  }
  return result
}
```

This can be used to convert [String:AnyObject] in the JSON function:

```
fn(toStringString(json))
```

The function can be tested with a test class using the data: protocol by passing in a **base64** encoded string representing the JSON data. To create a base64 representation, create a string, convert it to a UTF-8 data object, and then convert it back to a string representation with a data: prefix:

```
import XCTest
class NSURLExtensionsTest: XCTestCase {
  func testNSURLJSON() {
    let json = "{\"test\":\"value\"}".
     dataUsingEncoding(NSUTF8StringEncoding)!
    let base64 = json.base64EncodedDataWithOptions(nil)
    let data = NSString(data: base64,
     encoding: NSUTF8StringEncoding)!
    let dataURL = NSURL(string:"data:text/plain;base64,\(data)")!
    dataURL.withJSONDictionary {
      dict in
      XCTAssertEqual(dict["test"] ?? "", "value",
       "Value is as expected")
    }
  }
}
```

Parsing JSON arrays of dictionaries

A similar approach can be used to parse arrays of dictionaries (such as those returned by the list repositories resource). The differences here are the type signatures (which have extra square brackets `[]` to represent the array) and the fact that a **map** is being used to process the elements in the list:

```
func withJSONArrayOfDictionary(fn:[[String:String]] -> ()) {
  …
  if let json = NSJSONSerialization.JSONObjectWithData(
   data, options: nil, error: nil) as? [[String:AnyObject]] {
    fn(json.map(toStringString))
  } else {
    fn([[String:String]]())
  }
}
```

The test can be extended as well:

```
let json = "[{\"test\":\"value\"}]".
 dataUsingEncoding(NSUTF8StringEncoding)!
…
dataURL.withJSONArrayOfDictionary {
  dict in XCTAssertEqual(dict[0]["test"] ?? "", "value",
 "Value is as expected")
}
```

Creating the client

Now that the utilities are complete, the GitHub client API can be created. Once that is complete, it can be integrated with the user interface.

Talking to the GitHub API

A Swift class will be created to talk to the GitHub API. This will connect to the root endpoint host and download the JSON for the service URLs so that subsequent network connections can be made.

To ensure that network requests are not repeated, an NSCache will be used to save the responses. This will automatically be emptied when the application is under memory pressure:

```swift
import Foundation
class GitHubAPI {
  let base:NSURL
  let services:[String:String]
  let cache = NSCache()
  class func connect() -> GitHubAPI? {
    return connect("https://api.github.com")
  }
  class func connect(url:String) -> GitHubAPI? {
    if let nsurl = NSURL(string:url) {
      return connect(nsurl)
    } else {
      return nil
    }
  }
  class func connect(url:NSURL) -> GitHubAPI? {
    if let data = NSData(contentsOfURL:url) {
      if let json = NSJSONSerialization.JSONObjectWithData(
        data,options:nil,error:nil) as? [String:String] {
        return GitHubAPI(url,json)
      } else {
        return nil
      }
    } else {
      return nil
    }
  }
  init(_ base:NSURL, _ services:[String:String]) {
    self.base = base
    self.services = services
  }
}
```

As Swift 1.0 doesn't support conditional initializers, the pattern of using a class function to perform the initialization and return an optional value is a common one. With Swift 1.1, the implementation can be written as a convenience initializer init?, which can return an instance or nil.

This can be tested by saving the response from the main GitHub API site at `https://api.github.com` into an `api/index.json` file, by creating an `api` directory in the root level of the project and running `curl https://api.github.com > index.json` from a Terminal prompt. Inside Xcode, add the `api` directory to the project by navigating to **File | Add Files to Project...** or by pressing *Command + Option + A*, and ensure it is associated with the test target.

It can then be accessed with an `NSBundle`:

```
import XCTest
class GitHubAPITests: XCTestCase{
  func testApi() {
    let bundle = NSBundle(forClass:GitHubAPITests.self)
    if let url = bundle.URLForResource("api/index",
    withExtension:"json") {
      if let api = GitHubAPI.connect(url) {
        XCTAssertTrue(true,"Created API")
      } else {
        XCTAssertFalse(true,"Failed to parse \(url)")
      }
    } else {
      XCTAssertFalse(true,"Failed to find sample API")
    }
  }
}
```

> The dummy API should not be part of the main application's target, but rather of the test target. As a result, instead of using `NSBundle.mainBundle` to acquire the application's bundle, `NSBundle(forClass)` is used.

Returning repositories for a user

The APIs returned from the services lookup include `user_repositories_url`, which is a template that can be instantiated with a specific user. It is possible to add a method to the `GitHubAPI` class that will return the URL of the user's repositories as follows:

```
func getURLForUserRepos(user:String) -> NSURL {
  let userRepositoriesURL = services["user_repositories_url"]!
  let userRepositoryURL = URITemplate.replace(
```

```
    userRepositoriesURL, values:["user":user])
let url = NSURL(string:userRepositoryURL, relativeToURL:base)!
return url
}
```

As this might be called multiple times, the URL should be cached based on the user:

```
func getURLForUserRepos(user:String) -> NSURL {
  let key = "r:\(user)"
  if let url = cache.objectForKey(key) as? NSURL {
    return url
  } else {
    // acquire url as before
    cache.setObject(url, forKey:key)
    return url
  }
}
```

Once the URL is known, data can be parsed as an array of JSON objects using an asynchronous callback function to notify when the data is ready:

```
func withUserRepos(user:String, fn:([[String:String]]) -> ()) {
  let key = "repos:\(user)"
  if let repos = cache.objectForKey(key) as? [[String:String]] {
    fn(repos)
  } else {
    let url = getURLForUserRepos(user)
    url.withJSONArrayOfDictionary {
      repos in
      self.cache.setObject(repos,forKey:key)
      fn(repos)
    }
  }
}
```

This can be tested using a simple addition to the `GitHubAPITests` class:

```
api.withUserRepos("alblue") {
  array in
  XCTAssertEqual(22,array.count,"Number of repos")
}
```

> The sample data contains 22 repositories in the following file, but the GitHub API might contain a different value for this user in the future: `https://raw.githubusercontent.com/alblue/com.packtpub.swift.essentials/master/RepositoryBrowser/api/users/alblue/repos.json`.

Accessing data through the AppDelegate

When building an iOS application that manages data, deciding where to declare the variable is the first decision to be made. When implementing a view controller, it is common for view-specific data to be associated with that class; but if the data needs to be used across multiple view controllers, there is more choice.

A common approach is to wrap everything into a **singleton**, which is an object that is instantiated once. This is typically achieved with `private var` in the implementation class, with `class func` that returns (or instantiates on demand) the singleton.

> The Swift `private` keyword ensures that the variable is only visible in the current source file. The default visibility is `internal`, which means that code is only visible in the current module; the `public` keyword means that it is visible outside of the module as well.

Another approach is to use the `AppDelegate` itself. This is in effect already a singleton that can be accessed with `UIApplication.sharedApplication().delegate`, and is set up prior to any other object accessing it.

The `AppDelegate` is used to store the reference to the `GitHubAPI`, which could use a preference store or other external means to define what instance to connect to, along with the list of users and a cache of repositories:

```
class AppDelegate {
  var api:GitHubAPI!
  var users:[String] = []
  var repos:[String:[String]] = [:]
  func application(application: UIApplication,
    didFinishLaunchingWithOptions: [NSObject: AnyObject]?)
   -> Bool {
   api = GitHubAPI.connect()
```

```
            users = ["alblue"]
            return true
        }
    }
```

To facilitate loading repositories from view controllers, a function can be added to `AppDelegate` to provide a list of repositories for a given user:

```
func loadRepoNamesFor(user:String, fn:()->()) {
    repos[user] = []
    api.withUserRepos(user) {
        results in
        self.repos[user] = results.map {
            (r:[String:String]) -> String
            in r["name"]!
        }
        fn()
    }
}
```

Accessing repositories from view controllers

In the `MasterViewController` (created from the **Master Detail** template; or a new subclass of a `UITableViewController`), define an instance variable `AppDelegate` that is assigned in the `viewDidLoad` method:

```
class MasterViewController:UITableViewController {
    var app:AppDelegate!
    override func viewDidLoad() {
        app = UIApplication.sharedApplication().delegate
        as? AppDelegate
        ...
    }
}
```

The table view controller provides data in a number of sections and rows. The `numberOfSections` method will return the number of users, with the section title being the username (indexed by the users list):

```
override func numberOfSectionsInTableView(tableView: UITableView)
    -> Int {
    return app.users.count
```

```
}
override func tableView(tableView: UITableView,
 titleForHeaderInSection section: Int) -> String? {
  return app.users[section]
}
```

The `numberOfRowsInSection` function is called to determine how many rows are present in each section. If the number is not known, `0` can be returned while running a background query to find the right answer:

```
override func tableView(tableView: UITableView,
 numberOfRowsInSection section: Int) -> Int {
  let user = app.users[section]
  if let repos = app.repos[user] {
    return repos.count
  } else {
    app.loadRepoNamesFor(user) {
      Threads.runOnUIThread {
        tableView.reloadSections(
          NSIndexSet(index: section),
          withRowAnimation: .Automatic)
      }
    }
    return 0
  }
}
```

 Remember to reload the section on the UI thread, as otherwise the updates won't display correctly.

Finally, the repository name needs to be shown in the value of the cell. If a default `UITableViewCell` function is used, then the value can be set on the `textLabel`; if it is loaded from a storyboard prototype cell, then the content can be accessed appropriately using tags:

```
override func tableView(tableView: UITableView,
 cellForRowAtIndexPath indexPath: NSIndexPath)
 -> UITableViewCell {
  let cell = tableView.dequeueReusableCellWithIdentifier(
    "Cell", forIndexPath: indexPath) as UITableViewCell
  let user = app.users[indexPath.section]
```

```
    let repo = app.repos[user]![indexPath.row]
    cell.textLabel.text = repo
    return cell
}
```

When the application is run, the list of repositories will be shown, grouped by the user.

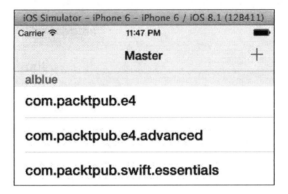

Adding users

At the moment, the list of users is hard-coded into the application. It would be preferable to remove this hard-coded list and allow users to be added on demand. Create an `addUser` function in the `AppDelegate` class:

```
func addUser(user:String) {
  users += [user]
  users.sort({ $0 < $1 })
}
```

This allows the detail controller to call the `addUser` function and ensure that the list of users is ordered alphabetically.

 The $0 and $1 are anonymous parameters expected by the sort function. This is a shorthand form of `users.sort({ user1, user2 in user1 < user2})`.

The add button can be created in the `MasterDetailView` in the `viewDidLoad` method, such that the `insertNewObject` method is called when tapped:

```
override func viewDidLoad() {
  super.viewDidLoad()
  let addButton = UIBarButtonItem(barButtonSystemItem: .Add,
   target: self, action: "insertNewObject:")
  self.navigationItem.rightBarButtonItem = addButton

  ...
}
```

When the add button is selected, a `UIAlertView` dialog can be shown with a `delegate` that will be called back to add the user. As before, the delegate must maintain a reference to itself until it completes, as otherwise, the object will be deallocated immediately.

 There is a replacement for `UIAlertView` in iOS 8 called `UIAlertController`. This can be considered if iOS 8 and above are being targeted.

Add (or replace) the `insertNewObject` function in the `MasterViewController` as follows:

```
func insertNewObject(sender: AnyObject) {
  let alert = UIAlertView(title: "Add user",
   message: "Please select a user to add",
   delegate: AddAlertDelegate(app,tableView),
   cancelButtonTitle: "Cancel",
   otherButtonTitles: "Add")
  alert.alertViewStyle = .PlainTextInput
  alert.textFieldAtIndex(0)?.placeholder = "Username"
  alert.show()
}
```

The AddAlertDelegate performs two functions; when completed, it calls the addUser on the AppDelegate; and secondly, it invokes the reloadData on the table, which ensures that the data is correctly shown. To do this, the delegate needs to have references to both the app delegate and the tableView, which are passed in the initializer:

```
class AddAlertDelegate: NSObject, UIAlertViewDelegate {
  var capture:AddAlertDelegate?
  var tableView:UITableView
  var app:AppDelegate
  init(_ app:AppDelegate,_ tableView:UITableView) {
    self.app = app
    self.tableView = tableView
    super.init()
    capture = self // prevent immediate deallocation
  }
  func alertView(alertView: UIAlertView,
   clickedButtonAtIndex buttonIndex: Int) {
    if buttonIndex == 1 {
      if let user = alertView.textFieldAtIndex(0)?.text {
        app.addUser(user)
        Threads.runOnUIThread {
          self.tableView.reloadData()
        }
      }
    }
    capture = nil
  }
}
```

Now the users can be added in the UI by clicking the add (+) button on the top-right of the application. Each time the application is launched, the users array will be empty, and users can be re-added.

 Users could be persisted between launches using NSUserDefaults. standardUserDefaults and the setObject:forKey and stringArrayForKey methods. The implementation of this is left to the reader.

Implementing the detail view

The final step is to implement the detail view, so that when a repository is selected per-repository information is shown. At the time the repository is selected from the master screen, the username and repository name are known. These can be used to pull more information from the repository and add items into the detail view.

Update the view in the storyboard to add four labels and four label titles for username, repository name, number of watchers, and number of open issues. Wire these into outlets in the DetailViewController:

```
@IBOutlet weak var userLabel: UILabel?
@IBOutlet weak var repoLabel: UILabel?
@IBOutlet weak var issuesLabel: UILabel?
@IBOutlet weak var watchersLabel: UILabel?
```

To set content on the details view, `user` and `repo` will be stored as (optional) strings, and the additional `data` will be stored in string key/value pairs. When they are changed, the `setupUI` method should be called to redisplay content:

```
var user: String? { didSet { setupUI() } }
var repo: String? { didSet { setupUI() } }
var data:[String:String]? { didSet { setupUI() } }
```

The `setupUI` call will also need to be called after the `viewDidLoad` method is called, to ensure that the UI is set up as expected:

```
override func viewDidLoad() { setupUI() }
```

In the `setupUI` method, the labels might not have been set, so they need to be tested with an `if let` statement before setting the content:

```
func setupUI() {
   if let label = userLabel { label.text = user }
   if let label = repoLabel { label.text = repo }
   if let label = issuesLabel {
     label.text = self.data?["open_issues_count"]
   }
   if let label = watchersLabel {
     label.text = self.data?["watchers_count"]
   }
}
```

If using the standard template, the `splitViewController` of the `AppDelegate` needs to be changed to use `return true` after the detail view is amended:

```
func splitViewController(
 splitViewController: UISplitViewController,
 collapseSecondaryViewController
   secondaryViewController:UIViewController!,
 ontoPrimaryViewController
   primaryViewController:UIViewController!) -> Bool {
   return true
}
```

 `splitViewController:collapseSecondaryViewController` determines whether or not the first page shown is the master (`true`) or detail (`false`) page.

Transitioning between the master and detail views

The connection between the master view and the detail view is triggered by the showDetail segue. This can be used to extract the selected row from the table, which can then be used to extract the selected row and section:

```
override func prepareForSegue(segue: UIStoryboardSegue,
  sender: AnyObject?) {
  if segue.identifier == "showDetail" {
    if let indexPath = self.tableView.indexPathForSelectedRow() {
      // get the details controller
      // set the details
    }
  }
}
```

The details controller can be accessed from the segue's destination controller — except that the destination is the navigation controller, so it needs to be unpacked one step further:

```
// get the details controller
let controller = (segue.destinationViewController as
  UINavigationController).topViewController
  as DetailViewController
// set the details
```

Next, the details need to be passed in, which can be extracted from the indexPath as in the prior parts of the application:

```
let user = app.users[indexPath.section]
let repo = app.repos[user]![indexPath.row]
controller.repo = repo
controller.user = user
```

The data needs to be acquired asynchronously using the withUserRepos method created previously. As this returns an array of repositories, it is necessary to filter out the one with the desired name:

```
app.api.withUserRepos(user) {
 repos -> () in
  controller.data = repos.filter({$0["name"] == repo}).first
}
```

Finally, to ensure that the application works in split mode with a `SplitViewController`, the back button needs to be displayed if in split mode:

```
controller.navigationItem.leftBarButtonItem =
 self.splitViewController?.displayModeButtonItem()
controller.navigationItem.leftItemsSupplementBackButton = true
```

Running the application now will show a set of repositories and when one is selected, the details will be shown:

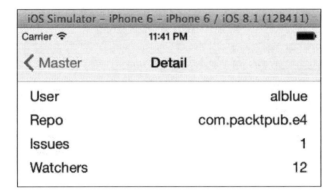

If a crash is seen when displaying the detail view, check in the `Main.storyboard` that the connector for a non-existent field is not defined. Otherwise, an error similar to **this class is not key value coding-compliant for the key detailDescriptionLabel** might be seen, which is caused by the Storyboard attempting to assign a missing outlet in the code.

Loading the user's avatar

The user might have an avatar or icon that they have uploaded to GitHub. This information is stored in the user info, which is accessible from a separate lookup in the GitHub API. Each user's avatar will be stored as a reference with `avatar_url` in the user info document such as `https://api.github.com/users/alblue`, as follows:

```
{
  ...
  "avatar_url": "https://avatars.githubusercontent.com/u/76791?v=2",
  ...
}
```

This URL represents an image that can be used in the header for the user's repository.

To add support for this, the user info needs to be added to the `GitHubAPI` class:

```
func getURLForUserInfo(user:String) -> NSURL {
  let key = "ui:\(user)"
  if let url = cache.objectForKey(key) as? NSURL {
    return url
  } else {
    let userURL = services["user_url"]!
    let userSpecificURL = URITemplate.replace(userURL,
     values:["user":user])
    let url = NSURL(string:userSpecificURL, relativeToURL:base)!
    cache.setObject(url,forKey:key)
    return url
  }
}
```

This looks up the `user_url` service from the GitHub API, which returns the following URI template:

```
"user_url": "https://api.github.com/users/{user}",
```

This can be instantiated with the user, and then the image can be loaded asynchronously:

```
import UIKit
...
func withUserImage(user:String, fn:(UIImage -> ())) {
  let key = "image:\(user)"
  if let image = cache.objectForKey(key) as? UIImage {
    fn(image)
  } else {
    let url = getURLForUserInfo(user)
    url.withJSONDictionary {
      userInfo in
      if let avatar_url = userInfo["avatar_url"] {
        if let avatarURL = NSURL(string:avatar_url,
          relativeToURL:url) {
          if let data = NSData(contentsOfURL:avatarURL) {
            if let image = UIImage(data: data) {
              self.cache.setObject(image,forKey:key)
              fn(image)
} } } } } } }
```

Once the support to load the user's avatar has been implemented, it can be added to the view's header to display in the user interface.

Displaying the user's avatar

The table view that presents the repository information by user can be amended so that along with the user's name, it also shows their avatar at the same time. Currently this is done in the `tableView:titleForHeaderInSection` method, but an equivalent `tableView:viewForHeaderInSection` method is available that provides more customization options.

Although the method signature indicates that the return type is `UIView`, in fact it must be a subtype of `UITableViewHeaderFooterView`. Unfortunately there is no support for editing or customizing these in Storyboard, so they must be implemented programmatically.

To implement the `viewForHeaderInSection` method, obtain the username as before, and set it to the `textLabel` of a newly created `UITableViewHeaderFooterView`. Then, in the asynchronous image loader, create a frame that has the same origin but a square size for the image, and then create and add the image as a subview of the header view. The method will look like:

```
override func tableView(tableView: UITableView,
  viewForHeaderInSection section: Int) -> UIView? {
  let cell = UITableViewHeaderFooterView()
  let user = app.users[section]
  cell.textLabel.text = user
  app.api.withUserImage(user) {
    image in
    let minSize = min(cell.frame.height, cell.frame.width)
    let squareSize = CGSize(width:minSize, height:minSize)
    let imageFrame = CGRect(origin:cell.frame.origin,
      size:squareSize)
    Threads.runOnUIThread {
      let imageView = UIImageView(image:image)
      imageView.frame = imageFrame
      cell.addSubview(imageView)
      cell.setNeedsLayout()
      cell.setNeedsDisplay()
    }
  }
  return cell
}
```

Now when the application is run, the avatar will be shown overlaying the user's repositories.

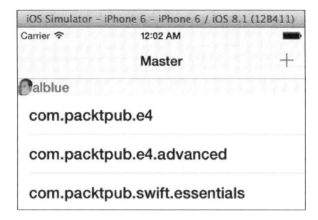

Summary

This chapter has shown how to integrate the subjects created in this book to integrate into a functional application for interacting with a remote network service such as GitHub and be able to present that information in a tabular way.

By ensuring that all network requests are implemented on background threads, and returned data is updated on the UI thread, the application will remain responsive to the user's input. Graphics and custom views can be created to provide headings, or the Storyboard could be modified to include more graphics for each repository.

Appendix

Learning any language initially focusses on the syntax and semantics of the language, but it quickly moves on to learning the suite of both standard and additional libraries that allow programmers to be productive. A single book cannot hope to list all the possible libraries that will be needed; this book is intended to be the start of a learning journey.

For further reading, this appendix presents a number of additional resources that might be useful to the reader in order to continue the journey. In addition, look out for other books by Packt Publishing that present the different aspects of Swift. This list of resources is necessarily incomplete; new resources will become available after the publication of this book, but you might be able to find new developments as they occur by following the feeds and posts of the resources below.

Language

The Swift language is developed by Apple, and a number of documents are available from the Swift developer page at `https://developer.apple.com/swift/`. This includes a language reference guide and an introduction to the standard library:

- The Swift programming language: `https://developer.apple.com/library/ios/documentation/Swift/Conceptual/Swift_Programming_Language/`

- The Swift standard library reference: `https://developer.apple.com/library/ios/documentation/General/Reference/SwiftStandardLibraryReference/`

- Integrating Swift and Cocoa: `https://developer.apple.com/library/ios/documentation/Swift/Conceptual/BuildingCocoaApps/`

- Swifter provides a list of all the Swift functions: `http://swifter.natecook.com`

Twitter users

There are a lot of active Twitter users who use Swift; in many cases, posts will be marked with the `#swift` hashtag and can be found at `http://twitter.com/search?q=%23swift`. Popular users that the author follows include (in an alphabetical order of their Twitter handle names):

- `@AirspeedSwift`: A good selection of tweets and re-tweets of Swift-related subjects
- `@ChrisEidhof`: The author of the *Functional Swift* book and `@objcio`
- `@CodeWithChris`: A collection of tutorials on iOS programming
- `@CodingInSwift`: Crossposts by a collection of Swift resources
- `@CompileSwift`: Posts on Swift
- `@cwagdev`: Chris Wagner writes some of the iOS tutorials with Ray Wenderlich
- `@FunctionalSwift`: A selection of functional snippets along with a *Functional Swift* book
- `@LucasDerraugh`: The creator of video tutorials on YouTube
- `@NatashaTheRobot`: A great summary of what's happening along with newsletters and cross references
- `@nnnnnnnn`: Nate Cook, who reviewed this book and provides the Swifter list above
- `@PracticalSwift`: A good collection of blog posts that talk about the Swift language
- `@rwenderlich`: Ray Wenderlich has many posts related to iOS development, a wealth of information, and more recently Swift topics as well
- `@SketchyTech`: A collection of blog posts on Swift
- `@SwiftCastTV`: Video tutorials of Swift
- `@SwiftEssentials`: The Twitter feed for this book
- `@SwiftLDN`: Swift meetups based in London, who also invite great Swift talks and presenters

In addition to the Swift-focused Twitter users, there are a number of other Cocoa (Objective-C) developers who blog regularly on topics related to the iOS and OSX platforms. Given that any Objective-C framework can be integrated into a Swift app (and vice versa), quite often there will be useful information that you can get by reading these posts:

- `@Cocoanetics`: Oliver Drobnik writes about iOS and provides training
- `@CocoaPods`: CocoaPods is a dependency management system for Objective-C frameworks (pods) and is being extended into the Swift domain
- `@Mattt`: Matt Thompson writes about many iOS subjects and is the author of the AFNetworking and Alamofire networking libraries
- `@MikeAbdullah`: Mike Abdullah writes about general iOS development
- `@MikeAsh`: Mike Ash knows everything there is to know, and for what he doesn't know, he finds out
- `@MZarra`: Marcus S Zarra has written a lot about Core Data and syncing
- `@NSHipster`: A collection of assembled iOS and Cocoa posts, organized by Matt Thompson
- `@objcio`: A monthly publication on Objective-C topics, with some Swift
- `@PerlMunger`: Matt Long posts about Swift, Cocoa, and iOS

The reviewers of this book are:

- `@AnilVrgs`: Anil Varghese
- `@ArvidGerstmann`: Arvid Gerstmann
- `@jiaaro`: James Robert
- `@nnnnnnnn`: Nate Cook

The author's personal and book twitter accounts are:

- `@AlBlue`: The author's twitter account
- `@SwiftEssentials`: The book's twitter account

Meetups such as `@SwiftLdn` keep a track of interesting Swift writers in a Twitter list at `https://twitter.com/SwiftLDN/lists/swift-writers/members`, which might have more up-to-date recommendations than this section, as well as of the Ray Wenderlich team at `https://twitter.com/rwenderlich/lists/raywenderlich-com-team/members`.

Blogs and tutorial sites

- `https://developer.apple.com/swift/blog/`: This is the official Apple Swift blog

- `http://airspeedvelocity.net`: This is the blog for `@AirspeedSwift`

- `http://alblue.bandlem.com/Tag/swift/`: This is the author's blog on Swift

- `http://mikeabdullah.net`: This is Mike Abdullah's blog

- `http://mikeash.com`: Here, you can find the Friday Q&A series on all things iOS and OSX

- `http://natecook.com/blog/tags/swift/`: This is Nate Cook's blog on Swift

- `http://nshipster.com`: This is the blog for `@NSHipster`

- `http://objc.io`: This is the blog for `@objcio`

- `http://practicalswift.com`: This is collected by `@PracticalSwift`

- `http://sketchytech.blogspot.co.uk`: This is a collected blog of Swift articles by `@SketychTech`

- `http://swiftnews.curated.co`: This is collected by `@NatashaTheRobot`

- `http://www.cimgf.com`: This presents a collection of topics on Cocoa, by Marcus S Zarra and others

- `http://www.raywenderlich.com`: This has a collection of tutorials about iOS development, including both Cocoa and Swift

Meetups

A number of local iOS developer groups existed before Swift was created; they have since then been supplanted by Swift-specific groups. These will, of course, vary by geographic location, but a few meetup sites exist such as Eventbrite at `http://www.eventbrite.co.uk` and Meetup at `http://www.meetup.com`.

It is also likely that there are Twitter groups or meetups near you; for example, in London, there is `@SwiftLDN` at `https://twitter.com/SwiftLDN` who have regular meetings listed at `http://www.meetup.com/swiftlondon/`. In New York, the `http://www.meetup.com/NYC-Swift-Developers/` group is fairly active. In San Francisco, both `http://www.meetup.com/swift-language/` and `http://www.meetup.com/San-Francisco-SWIFT-developers/` are active.

Afterword

A journey of a thousand miles begins with a single step. Your journey to writing great Swift applications has just begun. As with any journey, traveling companions can provide support, assistance, and encouragement, and many of the companions listed here can provide connections to many more. I hope you enjoy your journey.

Index

C

D

detail view
  implementing 189, 190
DetailViewController class 74-81
dictionary, collection types 12
direct network connections
  about 152
  asynchronous reading 162
  asynchronous writing 162
  stream connection, opening 153
  synchronous reading 154
  synchronous writing 154
documentation header
  entries, adding 54, 55
documentation section, playground
  adding 51, 52
  styling 53
document outline 89
drawRect
  graphics, drawing in 125
  used, for implementing
    custom graphics 123, 124
dynamic property content 110

E

enum (enumeration), Swift
  associated values 71
  creating 70
  raw values 70
equality operator
  differentiating, with identity operator 16
Eventbrite
  URL 200
expression list 22
extension 153
external parameter name 24

F

fill color 125
floating point literals 9
for loops
  iteration, using with 21
functions, Swift
  anonymous arguments 26
  arguments 26
  creating 23
  default values 25

  multiple return values 26
  named arguments 24
  optional arguments 25
  structured values, returning 29

G

getter (accessor) 66
GitHub API
  overview 171
  repositories resource 173
  root endpoint 172
  URL 171, 181
  user resource 172
GitHub repository
  URL 74
git protocol
  implementing 158, 159
git references
  remote listing 160, 161
Grand Central Dispatch (GCD) 143

H

half-open range, Swift range operators 18
hashbang 31
hole 142
HTTP
  URL 137
Human Interface Guidelines (HIG) 85

I

identifier 113
identity operator
  differentiating, with equality operator 16
if statement 15, 16
image asset files 60
images
  displaying, with QuickLook 42
Info.plist file 60
initial view controller 86
inout argument 146
interface builder
  actions, calling from 97, 99
  files 60
  used, for creating custom views 110

S

**Thank you for buying
Swift Essentials**

About Packt Publishing

Packt, pronounced 'packed', published its first book, *Mastering phpMyAdmin for Effective MySQL Management*, in April 2004, and subsequently continued to specialize in publishing highly focused books on specific technologies and solutions.

Our books and publications share the experiences of your fellow IT professionals in adapting and customizing today's systems, applications, and frameworks. Our solution-based books give you the knowledge and power to customize the software and technologies you're using to get the job done. Packt books are more specific and less general than the IT books you have seen in the past. Our unique business model allows us to bring you more focused information, giving you more of what you need to know, and less of what you don't.

Packt is a modern yet unique publishing company that focuses on producing quality, cutting-edge books for communities of developers, administrators, and newbies alike. For more information, please visit our website at www.packtpub.com.

Writing for Packt

We welcome all inquiries from people who are interested in authoring. Book proposals should be sent to author@packtpub.com. If your book idea is still at an early stage and you would like to discuss it first before writing a formal book proposal, then please contact us; one of our commissioning editors will get in touch with you.

We're not just looking for published authors; if you have strong technical skills but no writing experience, our experienced editors can help you develop a writing career, or simply get some additional reward for your expertise.

Xamarin Mobile Application Development for iOS

ISBN: 978-1-78355-918-3   Paperback: 222 pages

If you know C# and have an iOS device, learn to use one language for multiple devices with Xamarin

1. A clear and concise look at how to create your own apps, building on what you already know of C#.

2. Create advanced and elegant apps by yourself.

3. Ensure that the majority of your code can also be used with Android and Windows Mobile 8 devices.

Learning iPhone Game Development with Cocos2D 3.0

ISBN: 978-1-78216-014-4   Paperback: 434 pages

Harness the power of Cocos2D to create your own stunning and engaging games for iOS

1. Find practical solutions to many real-world game development problems.

2. Create games from start to finish by writing code and following detailed step-by-step instructions.

3. Full of illustrations and diagrams, practical examples, and tips for deeper understanding of game development in Cocos2D for iPhone.

Please check **www.PacktPub.com** for information on our titles

iOS Development with Xamarin Cookbook

ISBN: 978-1-84969-892-4   Paperback: 386 pages

Over 100 exciting recipes to help you develop iOS
applications with Xamarin

1. Explore the new features of Xamarin and learn
   how to use them.

2. Step-by-step recipes give you everything you
   need to get developing with Xamarin.

3. Full of useful tips and best practices on creating
   iOS applications.

Cocos2d-x Game Development Essentials

ISBN: 978-1-78398-786-3   Paperback: 136 pages

Create iOS and Android games from scratch
using Cocos2d-x

1. Create and run Cocos2d-x projects on iOS and
   Android platforms.

2. Find practical solutions to many real-world
   game development problems.

3. Learn the essentials of Cocos2d-x by writing
   code and following step-by-step instructions.

Please check **www.PacktPub.com** for information on our titles

Made in the USA
Lexington, KY
29 March 2015